Wedding Belles

How to make your dream wedding come true

From the creators of ConnectedWeddings.com

With photographs by Sephi Bergerson
Design and illustrations by Heema Sabharwal

RANDOM HOUSE INDIA

Published by Random House India in 2008
13579108642

Random House Publishers India Private Limited,
MindMills Corporate Towers, 2nd Floor,
Plot 24A, Sector 16A, Noida, U.P. 201301

Random House Group Limited, 20 Vauxhall Bridge Road, London SW1V 2SA, United Kingdom

978 81 8400 040 5

Printed and bound in India by Ajanta Offset

Getting Started 5

We've Only Just Begun: *Wedding Planning Fundamentals* 21

Getting the Wedding Belle Look 63

Where's the Party Tonight: *Pre-Wedding Events* 115

The Main Event 163

Behind the Scenes: *Working With Your Vendors* 195

Sailing Away: *The Honeymoon* 233

Happily Ever After: *Your Post-Wedding Life Together* 243

Appendix: *Reccomended Vendor Listings* 264

Index 283

Getting Started

You're a bride!

You've dreamt that it might happen, ever since you two laid eyes on each other at that coffee shop. (You were double espresso. He was the milky chai.) And then at the bookstore. (You were by the chick lit. He was reading Dalrymple.) When he got up the nerve to say hello, you found you had loads in common and you've been inseparable ever since. Your family loves him, and his can't get enough of you. You jumped up and screamed the night he popped the question. And you're still jumping up and down, when you think no one's looking.

Or, maybe you and your fiancé are new to the relationship game. Your parents hooked you up, and then left it up to the two of you. Hesitantly, you met for dinner—and ended up talking for hours You both felt a spark, something magical that let you know this was the man you wanted to watch sappy movies with, laugh at bad jokes with, and share your heart with. You made the match official and now you're moving quickly towards a big wedding.

Either of these stories sounds familiar? Or did you have a different kind of proposal? Whatever your personal road was, you're getting married! It couldn't be a more exciting time to be a bride in India. Increasingly, the twenty-first century bride plays a larger role than brides before her did. Many brides find their own grooms, and some may even play the host and pay for their own weddings. Even in arranged marriages, or ones where the parents are footing the bills, there's a greater emphasis on getting the bride's opinion. And a different kind of wedding, where you wouldn't necessarily, like your parents would, stress about impressing new in-laws or outdoing the Guptas next door with imported flowers and more upmarket liquor at the open bar.

Many of today's brides want their weddings to feel personal, realising this is a once in a lifetime chance to have a party with all of their loved ones. The brides—and the grooms —want a wedding that feels like them. This might mean incorporating family recipes into

the buffet, a slideshow of baby pictures, or an offbeat costume bash for friends.
As well as being a showcase for modern luxuries, weddings in India are also an amazing coming together of new and/or Western customs with traditions that are centuries old. These traditions and rituals, whether based on religion or custom, are important parts of your wedding, the prelude to many happily married years together. Though it's easy to lose focus when you're worrying about the details of five days of parties, five hundred or more guests, decorations, catering, looking like a princess, handling your own family under stress—not to mention bonding with your new family.

That's why we, the team from ConnectedWeddings.com, set out to write a handbook for new brides – to walk you through everything in a stylish, logical, and fun way, and hopefully make what at first seemed completely daunting, straightforward, and manageable. And it's especially important to talk to real brides who've been in your shoes (or delicate wedding slippers). We couldn't help but be captivated by the stories of brides and newlyweds, along the way. A few of them recount their most memorable moments:

'The first time I saw my husband on my big day, our eyes twinkled.'

'At the first reception my father asked me to dance with him. He attempted a jive, but I am hopeless at it, so he led me patiently.'

'The unlimited shopping! No seriously, I think the fact that some of my closest friends went through all kinds of trouble to fly in from different parts of the world for my D-Day. That was really touching.'

'My husband danced alone for me, pointing and singing aloud –"Main joru ka ghulam ban ke rahoonga," and we did a ball dance alone while everybody else watched.'

'The church ceremony where the priest asked us to hold hands, and we just continued holding hands even after.'

'When it was all over and we finally spent quality time together on the wedding night.'

You won't be able to plan which wedding moments will stand out. You may get overwhelmed at some point, when it hits you that you're surrounded and supported by all your loved ones. Or something will click when you realise that your fiancé is now your husband and you couldn't feel luckier. It might be something unexpected – a surprise dance by all your cousins at the sangeet, or your parents surprising you with a family heirloom emerald set that goes perfectly with your wedding sari, just like in a desi jewellery ad – when you realise that all those hours of planning were worth it. You can't choreograph every aspect of your wedding – and trust us, you won't want to – but you can think through the details in advance.

This book speaks to the bride who is the main orchestrator of her wedding. We realise that not every bride who reads this will be in charge of every aspect of her wedding, and some may be handing most of the responsibility over to parents. But all of our advice can be adapted to help the bride or her family; or to help the bride help her family.

A few points of clarification about how to use *Wedding Belles*. This book is meant to provide a framework for your thinking and planning. Every bride's situation, tastes, and resources will be different, so there's no way we could write an exact wedding plan that suits everyone. (That's why many brides who want a custom plan hire a wedding planner!) We recommend reading this book and combining it with your own thoughts and experiences to come up with ideas and refine your decision-making process.

Each bride's organisational style and tastes are going to be different. So as you flip through our recommendations for planning tips or even specific vendors, follow up with your own first-hand research – meet vendors face to face, see samples of their work, taste their food – to make sure that everything you choose is just right for you.

Champagne Wishes and Wedding Dreams: Your Wedding Vision

Now that you're a bride, you'll never be able to look at a wedding the same way again. It's one thing to be a wedding guest, - but it's way different to be planning your own big day. From the minute you get engaged, the questions start – Where? When? What will I wear? And just try to go to a friend's wedding without turning into the biggest critic you know. Sure, it was nice, but you wouldn't have chosen that blue-and-green colour scheme.

What will your wedding look like? Your fiancé will possibly have his dream, your parents and his may also have strong opinions, and practicalities like costs, number of guests, and locations and vendors may influence your plans. But get started by putting together your own ideas. Before you can plan the details, you need to think about the big picture though– and it all starts with a vision.

Great br-ideas: Wedding movies inspiration

Want an extra reason to get in the wedding spirit? We've got just the thing for you. *Indian Express* film critic Shubhra Gupta shares her fave movies about love and marriage, guaranteed to put the sparkle in your eyes and a bounce in your step. Sip from your tall glass of khus sherbet or watermelon cooler, and trip the light fantastic with these gorgeous Bollywood brides.

Kuch Kuch Hota Hai (1998): Oh, Shah Rukh and Kajol. Dunking baskets, or dancing in the Scottish meadows, or gazing at each other when they meet after a gap of many years: young love at its most lively. Fave mo: right towards the end, new suitor Salman lets Kajol go back to old love Shah Rukh. Can you feel the love tonight? Banish all doubts, and pre-wedding nerves. Happily ever after is where you are headed for!

Dilwale Dulhaniya Le Jayenge (1995): Shah Rukh and Kajol, again. They meet in London, fall in love in the snowy reaches of Switzerland, and marry in good ol' Punjab. Take our word for it – there's never been a more winsome couple in the movies. And that song, '*Mehendi lagaa ke rakhna*' is the mehendi song of all time. Play it at yours.

Hum Aapke Hain Kaun...! (1994): Salman and Madhuri create magic in this iconic movie, which unspools like an extended wedding video. Watch out for '*Didi tera dewar deewana*', the saucy song which had Madhuri in that famous purple choli: a billion brides got outfitted in exactly that colour, cut, and style.

Mere Yaar Ki Shaadi Hai (2002): It may be a rip-off of *My Best Friend's Wedding*, but this one is sure to make you smile just as much. Fresh-faced debutante Tulip Joshi and Jimmy Shergill as the couple-to-be, with Uday Chopra playing the spoiler old friend from the past. You know that true love will win, and that's always a blast.

Mujhse Dosti Karoge! (2002): Dreamboat Hrithik, quiet, intense Rani and bubbly, vivacious Kareena. Classic triangle, shot mostly in London: watch the threesome spar in one of the most picturesque cities of the world. Also look out for the unusual pastel-coloured lehenga-cholis Rani and Kareena wear at the engagement ceremony: pale pinks, and lilacs. Remember, this is your time to sigh over Hrithik all you like. Your spouse-to-be may not like the competition!

Jab We Met (2007): Remember when you literally fell into your boyfriend's arms, the first time you met? Did you chatter non-stop, and he looked at you, bemused and entranced? And remember how you had no idea at that time, but your girlfriends just knew that he was the man for you? Meet Shahid and Kareena in *Jab We Met*, one of Bollywood's freshest, sharpest rom coms—they go through just this routine and live to tell the tale happily after. Just what you are planning on!

Monsoon Wedding (2001): Is your house full of relatives, all talking at the same time, counting down to your big day? Your father busy finalising the tents, the flowers, and the shaadi ka khana? That hottie NRI from Australia crashing in the living room and romancing the family's flighty young thing – isn't that what's playing out in your house? And has your room been taken over by little cousins, all dying to be the bridesmaids and lead you out to the mandap? Sit all of them down, tell them to hush, and run *Monsoon Wedding*. So what if it isn't the monsoon just yet.

Do take the quiz in the following page – but now, close your eyes, and try to envision you and your fiancé getting married. Everything is perfect. Nothing is holding you back – cost, location, or family demands. It's just what appeals to you most. So think big and bold. Enjoy!

Once you come back to reality, jot down everything you remember. Where were you? Who was there? What did it look like? What was the vibe of the party? Chances are these first thoughts might be ingredients of the real thing. Maybe you'll have dreamed of being married in your temple, or out on an open lawn – this could help narrow down choices.

After you have the first vision details, compile your list bearing in mind your wedding priorities. Maybe you've always dreamed of getting married in a historic location, like a former palace. Or maybe you want the most inclusive wedding possible, with your and your fiancé's family's most extended circle.

To help you with your priorities list, consider these factors:
Time of the year: Is sweat-free winter weather a must, or have you always wanted a monsoon wedding à la Mira Nair?
Location: Close to home; at a favourite temple, farmhouse or hotel; at a landmark; or a destination wedding somewhere that has meaning for you and your fiancé. (A wedding overlooking the Taj Mahal for the seriously dedicated lovers amongst you, for example.)
Size: Just immediate family, up to everyone you've ever met.
Vibe of the party: Casual afternoon luncheon, fancy evening soirée, or glam modern do.
Decor: Do you have a favourite flower to set the scene; is there a wedding colour scheme that you've always been drawn to, a design element or theme that you've always wanted?

Now rank each entry. A – most important to your dream wedding, B – medium priority, or C – nice to have. Then take your list to your fiancé. You might want to ask him to go through the same exercise. Or if he's the type that likes to see you have a plan, then weigh in, go ahead and show him your list. Warning—you probably won't agree on everything!

Quiz: What type of wedding suits you best?

What you love most about your mate is:
a) He has the energy to hit every party with you on a Saturday night
b) He knows how to curl up with you, a good book, and a bottle of wine
c) He shares your passion for seeing the world
d) He shares your priorities, life plan

Your favourite part of school was always:
a) Drama class – you loved to put on a show
b) Seminars with more one-on-one time with your professor
c) Geography class – you were fascinated by different places and people
d) Economics – practical knowledge you knew you'd have a use for

In 'Friends', you identify most with:
a) Monica
b) Ross
c) Rachel
d) Phoebe

On a Saturday night with girlfriends you:
a) Party! Dinner and dancing at the hottest places in town
b) Have a cosy gab session at home
c) You already left in the morning for a hill station none of you've been to
d) Poetry reading or animal rights rally

For you, taking a risk means:
a) Throwing a soirée with friends from different circles; you know it'll work
b) Taking the microphone at karaoke night – the solo act isn't your thing
c) Doing a safari – sans travel guide
d) Going over your credit card limit

Stranded on a desert island you'd:
a) Bring all of your family and friends, and set up a mecca for island nightlife
b) Take your fiancé and your parents, photo albums and family heirlooms
c) Be filled with excitement. You can't pass up an adventure
d) Bring a raft, radios, satellite phones, and a detailed plan on how to get home

Mostly a: You're the perfect bride for a big fat Indian wedding! You love a party, and if it's for you, all the better. It wouldn't be your wedding if you couldn't share it with a guest list that's practically the size of your city. You want to find deep meaning in it as well, by following every tradition and ritual you know of, combining the East and the West and everything in between—and leaving the town talking about your wedding in the days (or years) to come.

Mostly b: You're the type of bride who'll be most comfortable with a smaller wedding bash. It's important to you for the focus of the wedding to be on your marriage and the families. You're not really excited about being the centre of attention, and you'd much rather be among a smaller group where you know each guest really well, than to have invited the whole world. An intimate ceremony in your garden at home, or in a treasured setting familiar to the family would be perfect for you.

Mostly c: You're right for a destination wedding; you've got the travel bug – and you can't get enough stamps in your passport. Making a scene in your hometown isn't your thing. A more intimate affair in a wonderful location would hit the spot – and would give you your dream vacation with your fiancé and all your closest friends and family in one place.

Mostly d: If you could, you'd just register your marriage and get it over with – you're not a party girl, and you're confident that the bond between you and your husband doesn't need the glitz and glamour of a big Indian wedding to show it off. But since you're girding your loins to go through with it, you're going to do it your way – so you can still save, and make that down payment on your first home together. Short and sweet will do the trick —a one-day wedding with not too many frills attached.

Countdown to your wedding:

Here's our breakdown of approximately when you're supposed to do what between now and your big day. We've also included where to flip in the book for more information. Remember, each wedding plan is different – so use this as a guideline to make your own customised checklist to stay on top of all your wedding to-dos.

Six months prior (or as soon as you know you're getting married!)

- Take the time to map out your dream wedding vision. (pp 23-6)
- Tackle the building blocks of wedding planning decisions – make your budget, pick your wedding date, and draw up your guest list. Consider your pre-wedding parties at this time as well (if you're having any). (pp 31-52)
- Decide if you're going to hire a wedding planner, and if so, hire one quickly so they can jump in to help right away. (pp 212-14)
- Decide if you want to have a destination wedding—since that will impact all of the other decisions to come. (p 52)
- Send out 'Save the date' notices to any out-of-town guests who might need extra notice to make it to your events. (p 217)
- Make your plan for eating healthy, exercising, and getting proper sleep to help you look your best for the wedding. (pp 105-9)
- Start shopping for your trousseau and wedding outfits. Note that designer couture can take three to six months to execute. You can wait a few months if you're planning to buy ready-made and won't feel the need to check out every store in town (or make shopping trips in multiple towns). But either way, you'll need two or three fittings per outfit to get alterations just right – plus time to pick out the perfect jewellery, footwear, and lingerie to match each ensemble. (pp 67-100)
- Reserve hotel rooms or guest house accommodation for your out-of-town guests. (pp 59-62)

Five months prior

- Find the priest (if applicable). (p 166)
- Research and book the vendors you'll need for each wedding event: venue, caterers, decorators/florists, stationery designer/printer, and DJ/band. (You can start researching your photographer/video man, choreographer, and mehendi artist as well, though you won't need to book them right away.) If possible, you and each vendor should sign a contract and you might need to put down a deposit. (Behind the Scenes, pp 195-232)

Four months prior

- Meet with each of the vendors you've booked and make a plan for what needs to happen between now and the wedding. Create deadlines for both you and them in terms of when decisions have to be made, samples viewed and approved, and meetings held. (Behind the Scenes, pp 195-232)

Three months prior

- Begin shopping for gifts to exchange with the groom and his family at the wedding. (pp 193-4)
- Work with your priest to plan an event flow for your wedding ceremony, including a list of all the gear you'll need to bring for the rites. Organise a document that explains the wedding day timeline for you, the groom, and close relatives. You can use the same information to create a programme for your guests. (p 169)

Two months prior

- Have your first fittings with your tailor for all of your wedding outfits. (pp 76-8)
- Order any jewellery you're having custom-made, as it takes at minimum a fortnight to produce. (pp 90-7)

- Hire a stylist to do your hair and make-up on your wedding day (and for any other events as well.) Schedule a trial to make sure you're happy with the look in advance. (pp 101-4)
- Book a mehendi artist to do your henna at your mehendi party. Ask for a trial if you've never seen their work before and can't get a good feel from their portfolio. (pp 227-30)
- Book a DJ for any events that call for music. (pp 224-26)
- Book a choreographer to bring dancers to one of your events, or if you want help learning a family dance for the sangeet or a special first dance to perform with your groom. If you're the ones who'll be doing the dancing, make a schedule for rehearsals leading up to the performance. (pp 220-23)
- Give your Notice of Intended Marriage in writing to the Marriage Officer in the district where you or your groom have been living for at least 30 days. If there are no objections to your union, you'll come back 30 days later with three witnesses to solemnise your marriage. (pp 170-72)

Six weeks prior

- This is the latest you should make any drastic haircuts or try skin brightening or polishing treatments (if your dermatologist recommends them). You don't want to do anything closer to your wedding day if you're not positive about how it will turn out. (p110)
- Deliver your wedding cards to all of your guests 3–6 weeks before the wedding. (p 217)

One month prior

- Create your wish-list of gifts to share with your families, so they're prepared with good answers if anyone asks what you'd like as a wedding gift. (pp 190-1)
- Your sisters or girlfriends may throw you a hen party or bridal shower this month. If so, enjoy, be a good sport and be sure to thank everyone. (pp 129-143)
- Book your photographer/video man. Make sure they understand the schedule of events

for your wedding, the shooting style you're looking for, and who and what you want them to focus on. (pp 208-10)

- Return this month to the Marriage Office with three witnesses to solemnise your marriage. (pp 170-72)
- Confirm and approve any favours you're having a vendor produce to give away at your parties. (pp 231-32)

Three weeks prior

- Check back with all of your vendors to remind them about your wedding plans and make any final preparations.

Two weeks prior

- Have your final fittings for your wedding outfits. Your tailor should quickly make any last-minute small tweaks and then send you home with each masterpiece. (pp 77-8)
- Confirm the number of out-of-town guests you have coming and make sure you have enough rooms to accommodate them. You may have to contact a few who are slow to respond to your invitation.
- Meet your mehendi artist to go over the plan for your henna application. (pp 228-30)
- Meet your DJ to set your plan for what he's going to play at your bash. (p 226)

One week prior

- Start welcoming your out-of-town guests as they arrive. Make sure they have an itinerary of all the planned events and that a member of your extended family or friends' circle can serve as a point of contact on call to help anyone who needs assistance. (pp 59-62)

- Get all the parlour essentials out of the way: facial, waxing, threading, bridal massage. Manicures/pedicures can be done now if you're not going to be doing any work that can lead to chipping. Or move these appointments closer to the date of your first function. Indulge in a spa treatment or two as well. Though be careful not to try anything for the first time that could cause a rash or breakout on your face. (pp 110-14)

On the big day!

- Hair and make-up: get help from a trusted parlour, or do them yourself. (pp 101-05)
- Have a blast at your wedding!

Post-wedding

- Enjoy your honeymoon. (pp 239-41)
- Settle into your new home. (pp 256-58)
- Send thank you notes. (pp 245-48)
- Change your name and all documents/pieces of identification that use your maiden name. (pp 249-51)
- Organise your wedding photos and video and share them with family and friends. (pp 252-55)

Now that you've planned your countdown and compared your visions, figuring out where they overlap, it's time to start thinking about the practicalities – next chapter, please!

We've Only Just Begun

Wedding Planning Fundamentals

You can't wait to get hitched to your honey. You've had a vision of your dream wedding since you were a little girl, and you want to make it come to life. The excitement is tinged with a little trepidation, though. Where do you start? This is the point, traditionally, where the bride's and groom's parents take over (and in many Indian families they still do.) The bride's family hosts the ceremonies, and the groom's family plans a reception after the wedding to welcome the bride into their family. The bride and groom do as told and show up when and where they're supposed to. But a twenty-first century bride is no longer the coy wife-to-be peering out from under her ghunghat. You're probably playing a more active role, whether you and the groom are throwing your wedding all by yourselves or sharing the planning with family.

So dive into the details – at a pace based on how much lead time you have before the big day.

On its website, Mumbai and UK wedding coordinating firm Tania-Tapel says the average Asian wedding takes about 300 hours, just to plan. Jaswinder Singh, a wedding planner from Ferns N Petals Events and Weddings, Delhi, says it's possible to plan a wedding in six weeks, or even a fortnight if you're willing to make some compromises and work on a tight schedule. Another Delhi-based wedding planner, Neeta Raheja, recommends you give yourself a minimum of six well-planned months. But even if you do have ten months or a year to plan, you'd still need to stick to a schedule.

In this chapter, we'll help you get organised and figure out how to start making your dream wedding a reality. Even if you're leading the charge, wedding planning is never an individual sport. You're going to need people you can count on along the way, as well as processes for how you'll do research, keep track of information, make decisions, keep a timetable, and pull all the details together.

This way you'll be ready to tackle the core building blocks of wedding planning decisions: your budget, your wedding date, and your guest list.

The A-Team: Your Wedding Planning Support System

Your wedding will be one of the most enjoyable and emotional highlights of your life. It will also probably be the biggest party you ever planned (until now), as well as the largest financial expense you and your family have ever borne. So you're going to need help – and lots of it!

Even if you're voted 'Most Organised Employee' every year, a wedding, especially your own, will challenge your planning abilities and may well be more than you can handle alone. Keep in mind help doesn't just come in the form of a demand draft or throwing you a hen party. You're going to need your pals around you, whether to listen to you debate the merits of marigolds and tuberoses versus orchids and carnations, or to help open that bottle of wine at the end of a hard day.

Your fiancé

If you've known each other for years, your fiancé is probably your perfect foil, your best friend and your strongest supporter. You're going to need him now more than ever!

Wedding planning isn't every guy's favourite pastime. Your groom's excitement about getting married may make him willing to jump in and share the workload with you, if you're lucky. Or, if planning's not his thing, hopefully his role will be to happily accept your decisions and then say thank you (many times over). Either way, you're still going to need him as a sounding board for ideas, as half of a united front when you're dealing with both sets of parents, and as an outlet to soothe you and keep you sane along the way.

It's okay (and even expected) for you and your groom not to have the same wedding vision. You might have always wanted an enormous theme wedding, while he's dreamt of an intimate affair. Finding a way to work together is great practise for married life.

Your parents and in-laws

After you and your fiancé, both sets of parents are the most important people. In most cases, they'll be willing co-conspirators in the wedding planning process – and many parents would be hurt if you didn't want them to be. As early as possible, sit down with both sets of parents, either separately or all together, to share ideas and expectations for the wedding. Some subjects are difficult to broach, but it's important to make sure you all know what the others are thinking, who is planning and paying for what, what funds are available, and what religious and family traditions are important to both sides.

Grab a helping hand

It's nearly impossible for a bride to plan a wedding without co-planners So who should you ask to help besides your hubby-to-be and your parents? Any relatives and friends who have time, interest, and experience pulling off a wedding, plus relevant skills. (Wedding vendors will of course take on much of the work – see Behind the Scenes, pp 195-232) Your out-of-town cousin can collect addresses of long-lost relatives living near her. A recently married girlfriend can share the venues she considered for her own ceremony. And your aunt with the sophisticated palate will love accompanying you to the caterers

Sharing the planning with your loved ones

When delegating responsibilities, keep these tips in mind:

- Give very clear instructions and deadlines. Don't be afraid to step up to the plate and tell your team exactly what you want, if you know they can deliver.
- Keep the communication lines open. Ask for notice if anything changes in terms of the basic task or deadline, and check in with your helper on a regular basis.
- Be grateful, even if something doesn't turn out exactly the way you intended. Your friend or family member did save you the time and hassle (or attempt to).
- Compromise and tact are particularly important when your parents or in-laws are involved; a clash over a young, friends-only mehendi versus a grand bash, for example.
- Take a deep breath, ask yourself how set you are on your idea, and remember this is just one of many wedding planning match-ups. Have a confrontation only when crucial!

Great br-ideas: Don't do all your own shopping

If you're too busy to shop for your entire trousseau, let your mother and/or mother-in-law shop on your behalf (if they offer). Send them off with all your measurements and silk threads in your fave shades. Or, pick and choose; buy the saris for the ceremony and reception yourself, and they can pick the mehendi outfit.

Brides sometimes clash with their parents about who—and how many— to invite to their wedding. You may as well. If mom really wants her colleagues there, maybe she'll help you plan another event for your friends. If your original plan wasn't that important to you, maybe let her take over the mehendi planning while you relax and earn brownie points, keeping your opinions for something you feel more strongly about. Note: You'll want to be even more open to compromise if you're living far from home and just taking a couple of weeks off to get married in the city where your parents live.

When Mumbai magazine writer Rojita and her fiancé Bhasker, who works for a wealth management firm, married in February 2006, they had their marriage ceremony in her hometown in Orissa and reception in his hometown of Madhya Pradesh. The two sets of parents made all the arrangements (though the couple helped with the menu by phone), 'and we were not bothered for small things,' Rojita remembered. 'For us, it worked out well,' she said.

If your parents don't mind the extra work, letting them take charge might make for the easiest logistics. After all, they'll probably be inviting the majority of the wedding guests. So giving up control might be a blessing in disguise – you might feel almost like a favoured guest at your own wedding.

Wedding whisperers: Your stress soothers

Working hard on your wedding, worrying and losing sleep will only give you dark circles, so identify who and what destresses you best. Which family members and friends have a calming effect on you? You and your fiancé should take good care of yourselves and each other throughout your wedding planning journey. Whether you love to chill out at the movies, spa, gym, or over dinner with him, and be sure to schedule time to indulge. Psychiatrist Dr Veena Kapoor from Delhi advises brides, 'Focus on life after the wedding, too, to avoid the post-wedding blues.'

Planning Makes Perfect: Wedding Planning For Beginners

Ready to get started? Great. Now you need your planning basics. If you have all the details planned in advance, there's no reason to stress, right?

Just as there are different types of brides, there are different ways to go about planning your wedding. As you read through the categories below, think about your personality and lifestyle, and identify the method that suits you best. Also, you might want to plan with a mix of styles – which works well for many brides.

For instance, a small mehendi at home, but a large ceremony and reception at a rented venue. You can also switch it up in terms of who's at the helm; it's fine to hire a wedding planner to manage the larger functions, but then take on all the arrangements for the smaller mehendi party at home with just your family helping.

Style child: What's your wedding planning style?

Do-it-yourself: The crafty bride with a thousand talents to her credit. Have a passion and flair for arranging flowers, designing invites, make-up? You're the DIY bride.
What it entails: Taking on the planning and execution of the majority of what needs to be done. You'll dream up the vision for all of your events, zero in on what to do to make each perfect, and get cracking, hopefully with the help of family and friends. A word of warning: a DIY wedding is a lot of work, you may end up with too much on your plate.

Big picture: The bride who knows what she wants, but also knows how to delegate.
What it entails: You'll plan the vision for each of your functions, and then find and book the perfect venue, the best caterer, and a slew of other vendors to take over the execution of every detail. Your role then will be to coordinate between the professionals you've hired and make sure it all comes together according to your plan – just like you want it.

Package deal: The busy bride who's looking to make the most of her budget and time.
What it entails: You'll seek out venues and vendors that multi-task. Most hotels that hold weddings also provide food and drinks, and maybe even decorations and music as well through a pre-approved vendor. If you work with them, you're getting a team of vendors who've worked together and can negotiate for an all-inclusive price. Other vendors often double up too: some florists also handle lighting, and some make-up artists do hair and wardrobe styling—which helps coordinate your wedding look and saves time getting ready.

Wedding planner: Brides who have no idea where to start planning, comfortable in a professional's experienced hands; who want to pull off an elaborate theme that will be the talk of the city (think Bollywood retro glamour, Arabian Nights or a cigar lounge). Also if you don't have a lot of time to research each vendor yourself, or want an extra person involved with tasks and decision-making that might otherwise stress the family.
What it entails: They'll offer stress-free planning to suit your budget; help create a wedding vision, select and coordinate vendors, help you find ways to save. They'll even find you a much-needed spa service to keep you glowing before the big day! For full details on wedding planners, see our guide on pp 212-14.

Real Life Wedding Belles

Nisha and Sidhartha, 3 December, 2005, New Delhi

Nisha and Sidhartha met in London during their Freshers' Week at college and got married eight years later, when Nisha was working for her father's import and fishing trawler businesses in Mauritius. Sidhartha, a consultant with Accenture, was with his family in New Delhi, so his parents took over the arrangements for their 1,100-person bash at the Taj Palace. They hired Preeti Sandhu, a wedding planner who worked with Wizcraft, to help Nisha out with the final preparations.

'The wedding planner was a real help,' Nisha remembered, reminiscing about how when she arrived in Delhi, Preeti came by every morning with a list of all that needed to be done that day. 'Sometimes I feel I wouldn't be married today, if not for her,' Nisha said. 'I would have gone mad – nobody had warned me about the stress during preparations for the wedding-related ceremonies. She thought I was crazy, but handled it well.'

The two women became friends during the lead-up to the wedding so Nisha felt comfortable playing a joke on the planner on the wedding day. Nisha got stuck in traffic on the way back from the beautician, so when the baraat arrived, Preeti called to ask where she was. 'I told her I was running away, as I wasn't keen on going through with the marriage,' Nisha recalled, 'and she went ballistic.' They both laughed afterwards.

Two wedding anniversaries later, Nisha still has fond memories of how her wedding planner helped melt her stress away.

Early bird: Get organised

Are you one of those girls who scribble notes on scraps of paper? Or are you the tsarina of the spreadsheet, doing lists, events, and online reminders? Pick up a journal or notebook or try a Filofax-style binder that includes a calendar plus note sheets. Anything that keeps your info in one place, and fits into your purse. So what do you have to keep track of?

- Dates and times of all appointments and functions.
- To-do lists of what's left to accomplish, and what's been done. (See our wedding countdown to-do list on pp 15-20 and ConnectedWeddings.com to make a to-do list online.)
- Guest lists with addresses, invites and thank you notes sent, RSVPs and gifts received.
- Names and contact info of all of your vendors, notes from meetings with them.
- Guest accommodation and hosting information and details.
- Timelines for each of your wedding functions: mehendi, sangeet, reception etc.
- Budget for all of this!

Bookworm: Wedding research

- As a bride, you're following in the tradition of many, many women before you and they are excellent resources for ideas and guidance. Your doting aunt was a bride too, you know.
- Family elders – a super information bank on what's been done before (your nani's been to countless weddings by now), and how they've been done by your family.
- Recent brides – sisters, cousins, friends, friends of friends...
- Bridal magazines like *Vivaha, Wedding Affairs, Indiawali Brides, Asiana Brides, Bride and Style,* and *Me and My Wedding* (a Pakistani publication) show the latest bridal fashion trends, and discuss wedding planning. *Vogue* and *L'Officiel* also cover bridalwear trends.
- Websites – another place to look for articles and ideas.
- Bollywood and Hollywood films – another fun place for inspiration.

Easy as one, two, three: Wedding planning building blocks

The core of your wedding planning revolves around what we, *Wedding Belles*, call the building blocks of wedding planning decisions: your budget, wedding date, and guest list. Your budget, date, and guest list are also complicated because they're tied to each other. How much money you decide to spend will impact how many guests you can afford to have at your events. And the number of guests you want to host will, conversely, impact your budget. Another factor to keep in mind is time and dates: choosing the big, popular wedding dates will raise prices, and a shorter planning timeline will leave you less time to hunt for the best deals. The wedding date might also decide how many guests attend.

By the numbers: Setting the budget

You and your fiancé have dreamed up your perfect wedding, but before you make any firm plans, you need to answer this question: how's it going to get paid for?

Traditionally, the couple's parents paid for all of the wedding expenses. The bride's family would typically cover costs for the engagement, mehendi, sangeet, wedding ceremonies and meal. They'd also pick up the tab for lodging and boarding wedding guests, the bride's trousseau, gifts for the groom (like clothes, a watch, toiletries), and gifts for the groom's family. The groom's family would buy the bride clothes and jewellery, and then welcome her with a reception.

But more and more couples are falling in love and bringing their families together for a wedding, rather than the other way around, and these modern couples are setting the tone for who pays for what. The rules are being rewritten, often as families are dividing the bill based on what each side can afford, the couple themselves pay if they're earning well, or the two families split the costs down the middle. Modern brides and their families, when hosting, might even put limits on the number of guests the groom's family invites – a dramatic departure from the previous assumption that the groom's family was entitled to make unlimited demands.

So how do you decide who's paying for what? The first step is for you and your fiancé to talk to both sets of parents. Unless one or both families have a bottomless bank account, it may feel a bit uncomfortable to speak frankly about finances, but not knowing how much of a budget you have to work with could make for an even more uncomfortable situation down the line. Be sensitive, knowing that those who are chipping in will probably want to help decide how their money will be spent. Be gracious and inclusive – you might hurt feelings if you bluntly declare you'll top up the difference to do it your way.

If you're going the traditional route and your parents are the ones footing the wedding bill, this is the time to set the groom's side's expectations about what your family can spend on the wedding if they are to stay in their financial comfort zone. 'A discussion before the wedding with your in-laws is a must, to let them know your or your parents' capacity to spend,' advises Nalini Prabhu of Alacrity Securities and Odyssey Financial Services in Bangalore.

Other funding sources

Think beyond mom and dad – other members of your family can chip in for your wedding, too. If grandparents, aunts, uncles, or cousins generously offer to host a wedding event in full or in part, or make some other type of contribution towards your wedding, you can graciously accept. Also, friends of the family who feel like aunties might also be up to hosting the mehendi, or a meal for your out-of-town guests. You'll be glad you did, whether they offer to help with something big like throwing your entire sangeet, or something smaller like providing the flowers for that night or cash to make up your deficit. And, family members pitching in will feel more involved in your wedding.

Many couples and their families want to spend more than they can afford on weddings and end up falling into the trap of dipping deep into their savings, taking out personal loans, or counting on cash wedding gifts to pay their wedding bills. We strongly advise against any of these routes, as does investment consultant Nalini Prabhu.

'Cut the coat according to the cloth,' says Prabhu. 'Do not borrow for the purpose of the wedding. Invitees, venue, expenses for entertaining invitees, lights, flowers – should be governed by the amount you've set aside. Don't start off with debt! For you or your parents.' We especially discourage relying on cash gifts you may get at the wedding because you can't predict how many of your guests will gift you cash, or how much cash those guests will give. So do plan to set aside whatever cash you get for after the wedding – to help set up your new home or start saving for big purchases in your new married life.

Budgeting know-how

You'll want to make as accurate an estimate as possible, and then keep track of what you actually spend along the way. To get a picture of wedding expenses, see table, pp 36–9. Whether you're going to spend one month's salary or your entire savings on your wedding, here are some tips to help you make a plan you can stick to:

- Set an upper limit you're all comfortable with and commit to not going over.
- Create a contingency fund by setting aside 10–20% of your budget for surprises. You'll be glad you did when your guest list doubles, or when you fall for an extravagant outfit.
- Set your spending priorities for where you'd like to splurge, where you'd like to shell out just about the average of what you have to spend to get good quality goods and/or services, and where you might try to save a few bucks. Trade-offs are unavoidable.

Bridal outfits, hairstyling and make-up usually fall in the vital category, and many brides like to splurge on these to ensure they look perfect. Neha, a trained fashion designer who married in April 2007, knew her priority was the photography, so she felt good about hiring high-end photographer Ronicka Kandhari. 'Each of her pictures is like a work of art,' Neha recalled. 'I knew when I saw her work that she would not miss any important moment. I have blow-ups of my favourites and lovely albums full of pictures.' For another bride, Nisha, the emphasis was on her honeymoon in London, Paris, and Dubai, so she made that the wedding expense she budgeted for first.

Ask the experts

We asked certified financial planner Pramod Bajaj how he advises his clients in Delhi about weddings in their families.

How early should families speak with a financial adviser about how to pay for wedding expenses?

My clients sometimes ask for advice years before a wedding. In some communities, trust funds or other investments are made within months after a daughter's birth. Otherwise, lead time should be based on the budget of the wedding and the finances the family has available for that budget.

How far in advance of the wedding should families liquidate investments to pay for the wedding expenses?

Ideally, the family should initiate the process of liquidating real estate investment at least 12 to 18 months before funds are needed to avoid the situation of distress sale. If equity investments need to be cashed, I recommend the same amount of advance time, and then I'd help the family reinvest in safer outlets, like fixed bank deposits/money market mutual funds or fixed maturity mutual fund plans etc. to keep the money accessible, while still earning a small amount of interest, so it doesn't depreciate much due to inflation.

Liquidating of assets or loans – what do you suggest?

If you can find a loan that asks for a lower rate of interest than what you're earning on your investments, it makes financial sense to take out a loan and leave your investment untouched. Otherwise, liquidating a few assets is the less expensive way to go.

Fixing your budget: Calculate your expenses

Costs from both the bride's and groom's sides included

Category	Estimated cost	Actual cost
Stationery Invitation cards (for all events, including map etc.)		
Thank you cards		
Rooms, meals, and transportation for out-of-town guests		
*Pre-wedding ceremonies** Venue rentals		
Catering		
Liquor (optional		
Decorations		
Music (if applicable)		

* Multiply by the number of events you're hosting.

Category	Estimated cost	Actual cost
Event-specific services (choreographer, mehendi artist and favours)		
Bride's/Groom's dress and accessories		
Photography/video		
Miscellaneous		
Trousseau Clothes		
Accessories		
Houseware		
Jewellery (including engagement rings)		
Miscellaneous		

Category	Estimated cost	Actual cost
Wedding day Fee for priest		
Venue		
Decorations		
Catering		
Photography/video		
Bride's/Groom's dress and accessories		
Make-up and hairstyling (bride)		
Miscellaneous		
Reception Venue		

Category	Estimated cost	Actual cost
Decoration		
Catering		
Liquor		
Photography/video		
Music and/or entertainers		
Gratuities		
Wedding night hotel and honeymoon		
Gifts (groom's side, your family and others who've helped)		
Total		

Ask the experts

According to TJ Wedding Planners, Bangalore, an average budget for a wedding with a headcount of 500 (excluding the bridal jewellery) would be Rs 300,000. A major component is often the venue and catering.

Minakshi Gupta from Little Gestures wedding planners in Hyderabad says most wedding budgets get broken up in these percentages, as below:

Venue: 10%	Ambience: 10%
Entertainment: 10%	Food: 50%
Photography: 5%	Hospitality: 15%

Check out a sample budget on the next two pages, taken from real wedding belle, Ramneeta. Ramneeta, an MBA student, and her fiancé Ricky, an engineer, were both living in San Francisco, but held their February 2008 wedding in New Delhi for the convenience of both of their families. Ramneeta's family hosted a small mehendi party for her at home, as well as cocktails and the main wedding. The groom's side hosted a sagan ceremony.

We found that Ramneeta spent less than many Delhi brides usually do on her bridal attire and jewellery (only 7% of her total budget). But she spent a good amount on her gifts for the groom and his family (15% of her total budget).

While you may spend very different amounts than Ramneeta did in terms of percentages or actual figures, we recommend using her budget as a point of reference when planning your own. You can follow her percentages if you'd like, but then make sure to adjust based on your own wedding priorities.

Ramneeta's budget

Wedding stationery 300 invitations for Rs 85 each Rs 2,000 for courier expenses Rs 2,000 for boxes of sweets for hand-delivered cards	Rs 29,500 (2%)
Accommodation for out-of-town guests Hired a house	Rs 45,000 (3%)
Mehendiwali Included bride's mehendi and 30 guests' applications	Rs 14,000 (1%)
Cocktails Rs 1,000 per head for venue and catering for 100 guests	Rs 1,00,000 (6%)
DJ	Rs 20,000 (1 %)
Wedding catering Rs 1,500 per head for venue and catering for 700 guests	Rs 10,50,000 (60%)
Floral decorations and lighting Included all three events	Rs 25,000 (1%)

Photography and video Rs 10,000 for cocktails Rs 15,000 for sagan Rs 30,000 for wedding day	Rs 55,000 (3%)
Bridal attire for three functions Lehenga-choli to start with: Rs 30,000 Suit for pheras: Rs 20,000 Suit for doli: Rs 22,000	Rs 72,000 (4%)
Bridal jewellery Wedding day rental of imitation jewellery: Rs 7,000 Doli time purchase of gold set: Rs 50,000	Rs 57,000 (3%)
Make-up and hairstyling package Included pre-bridal trials and wedding day styling	Rs 15,000 (1%)
Gifts for groom	Rs 1,00,000 (6%)
Gifts for groom's family – clothes and jewellery	Rs 1,50,000 (9%)
Tips and gratuities	Rs 10,000 (1%)
TOTAL	Rs 17,42,500

Great br-ideas to splurge or save on

Splurge on:

* Wedding outfits in expensive fabrics from a brand name designer
* A special gift for your invitees – a keepsake, to remember your wedding
* A last-minute impromptu bash with your special friends
* Spa services to help you relax and beautify yourself before the wedding
* Professional performers at your sangeet
* Flair bartenders with mixology tricks, juggle with fire? Think Tom Cruise in *Cocktails*
* A celebrity DJ
* A more exotic and/or longer honeymoon
* Imported, out-of-season flowers; multi-cuisine buffets by top restaurant/caterer

Save by:

* Taking your time to shop around for your bridal outfits and have options to compare
* Buying fabric from a wholesale market and having your family tailor do the stitching
* Using the same vendors for more than one event to bargain for a better rate
* Having a daytime wedding to save on lighting
* Selecting a picturesque location that requires little decoration
* Using fewer/less expensive flowers in décor; supplementing with diyas, ribbons, fruit
* Serving just one cuisine or hiring one caterer with different cuisine options
* Closing the bar early during your sangeet/cocktail party to save on liquor costs
* Using your own CDs/ iPod instead of hiring a DJ, especially for smaller events like the mehendi (You can still rent a powerful audio system.)
* Having your wedding planner, if you hire one, shop for garlands, turbans and other items at wholesale prices, and give you other money-saving recommendations

Managing the moolah

After you make a budget, stick to it. How?

- Keep close tabs on the money you're spending and where it's going, so you can make sure you're not overspending, or make extra cutbacks if you are. If you find a few places to save along the way, you might even end up with some leftover cash at the end.
- One way to stay within your budget is to open and operate from a separate wedding bank account. You, your parents, and your fiancé may all be handing out advances to vendors. Using the same account will help you keep clean records, prevent duplicate payments, and make sure all the family involved know how much money is left.
- For cash expenses, you can keep a separate log. And if you're worried about overspending or misplacing cash, you might try dividing it into separate envelopes for each category of expense according to your budget. You could keep your spending log directly on the appropriate envelope, with your receipts and contracts inside.

Mark your calendar: Picking your wedding date

You've dreamed of the big day ever since you met your fiancé. Ideally, you'd pick the most convenient day for your wedding, but many brides also consult religious traditions.

For example, Muslim couples look to their lunar calendar and try to get married on their saad, or auspicious, dates. Sikhs and Christians hold weddings on Sundays, and Christians also sometimes leave enough time before the wedding to attend prenuptial counselling sessions with their priest (it's usually a weekend programme) so they can receive the certificate from the church they want to get married in. Hindu pandits will solemnise a wedding only during an auspicious time. To help select the right date, first an astrologer matches the bride's and groom's horoscopes, comparing their 36 attributes and looking for a minimum of 18 matches, then checking the couple's cosmic charts for inauspicious moments. 'Even for the best-matched horoscopes, if the cosmic bodies are not in a desirable alignment, marriage ceremonies are not advised,' explains M.L. Verma, an astrologer from Delhi. There are also a few days when there is no shaadi ka saaya. Once your priest, pandit, astrologer and/or family elders approve of a few potential wedding dates, you can pick the one that works best for you, the groom and the immediate families. (In some cases, you might want to check work schedules and other potential conflicts at the same time as you are considering auspicious dates.) You should also see if your favourite venues are available on any of your possible dates. And then think about which date will be easiest for your guests. Maybe a late December date would be best for your cousins at school abroad to travel home, or a Saturday night would suit your working friends. And a winter weeknight rather than a sweltering weekend in June!

The most popular days of the wedding season

Most brides choose to get married when the weather is cooler, but if there haven't been any auspicious dates for a considerable number of months, more couples are waiting for the right time, and they all end up getting married on the same auspicious date, and possibly at the same time even. In Delhi alone, records have been set in recent years with approximately 20,000 weddings all on a single day.

If you're sharing your wedding date with thousands of other couples in your city, know that crowds drive up competition, prices and cause various delays. Booking your preferred venue, decorator, caterers and music might be more difficult to arrange and could come at a higher price. When make-up artists get overbooked, they often can't come to your home, so you may need to travel to their studios through heavy traffic on the day of wedding. And the same traffic could possibly delay your groom's arrival, and your pandit and your guests who might not be able to stay as long as they would have otherwise because they have to hit multiple affairs on the same day.

But there's a bright side to having your shaadi during the height of the wedding season. You could plan for a shorter ceremony, knowing your pandit has to get to his next function. And you could invite a larger number of guests but keep in mind that they will most likely eat at one of the other weddings they're attending later that night!

Be our guest: Making your guest list

Contrary to what you might think, you don't have to invite every person you've ever met for your wedding. Invite the family and friends who mean the most to you. 'Close relatives and friends, people who matter to you, who have been in touch with you since childhood,' says etiquette consultant Rukshana Eisha.

The rest of your guest list depend on the size of your wedding, Eisha advises asking important members of your community, extended family, friends who've invited you for their weddings, your boss and colleagues. Your parents could be concerned about keeping numbers reasonable to stay within the budget, or fit into a particular wedding venue, and then find out your fiancé's parents want to invite double the number of guests they'd estimated.

One bride Nazia, a Bangalore-based sociology teacher who had several pre-wedding parties and over 1,500 guests including many business associates, local community members and social acquaintances of her parents, remembered that making her guest list was the only bit of her wedding planning she actually hated because of the long-drawn-out sessions she had to sit through, trying to include or eliminate people without hurting too many sentiments. Keep in mind that your families have probably been looking forward to your wedding for many years now. If tension strikes, do all you can to make sure everyone

Great br-ideas: Imagine the invitees in your shoes

If you're worried about offending a not-so-close friend by not inviting them for your bash, ask yourself if she or he would invite you for theirs Sometimes, the friend's wedding has already happened, and you'll have your answer immediately – but in the case of single friends who you're on the fence about, give it some thought. If they chose not to invite you, would you be offended?

comes away having had their basic expectations met, but having enjoyed the wedding. And lastly, they say you can't make everyone happy – but pre-wedding events offer that elusive chance for compromise, since you don't have to invite the same guests to your mehendi, sangeet or other events. You can use extra functions to have a more intimate gathering, or to include groups you can't fit into the other events. (For more ideas on pre-wedding event guests, see pp 117-20.)

Etiquette answers

Is it mandatory to invite my whole office?
No, though you should strongly consider inviting your boss – even if you're not particularly close, as s/he will be giving you time off for the wedding and honeymoon. Plus it could make your relationship stronger, which can't hurt you in terms of office politics and any recommendations you might ask for down the line. Of the rest of the bunch, just invite the colleagues you're close to outside of work, unless you are having a really large wedding.

Do I need to invite guests who most likely won't be able to travel in from far away?
Etiquette Consultant Rukshana Eisha suggests that a courtesy invitation is a nice gesture, even if you know that they may not make it from out of town.

How do you politely tell out-of-town family that you've decided to have a smaller wedding that doesn't include them?
You can let your extended group know about your wedding with a personal note and maybe a small token, box of sweets or even a CD with video showing the rites. (This approach works well if you have a small destination wedding as well.) If your reasons for the tight guest list are financial, explain that you would have loved to have them at the celebration, but that you and the groom kept things small to save up money for your new house together, your studies abroad, etc.

Guess who's coming for dinner?

No matter who's on your guest list, you'll need an estimate of who's going to be coming for which event to choose the right size venue, and to get a cost estimate with your caterer. While the cost of decoration might be the same irrespective of the total number of invitees, catering costs might increase substantially if the list gets longer. Don't leave yourself to guessing who'll turn up. Wedding planner Nishika Pawa recommends the following formula:

Estimated headcount = closest family and friends attending (+ additional guests – 30%)

Pawa also subtracts additional guests from the estimate if it's a season when there are simultaneous parties, or if the wedding itself has multiple events. If there are four events related to the wedding, all of your guests won't show up for all of them, she says. They'll choose the events that are most convenient for them, so the day of the week will be an important factor. Relatives and family friends who have known you for years are likely to come for all events. Your colleagues may come as a group for the larger events, as the mehendi or sangeet are considered a family affair; though the ones you're close to might come to the mehendi, and skip the big wedding day, where they won't know anybody.

You'll probably save money if you err on the side of confirming less guests than you'll have, rather than overshooting. Most caterers won't allow you to decrease the confirmed number of guests, but they'll welcome additions. The Panchshila Rendezvous banquet hall in Delhi always prepares enough food to easily serve up to 10% more guests than the hosts anticipate. After the event, they count the number of plates used to see if the family needs to pay for additional guests. (See pp 206-7 for more on working with caterers)

Nupur, a bride who got married in New Delhi in 2007, thought she was being savvy when she invited 700 guests to her wedding and then told the caterer that her count would be 600. (She knew the caterer could then feed up to 650 guests.) But Nupur's wedding was on a weekday, and only 500 people ended up coming. So she and her family still had to pay the caterer to for 600.

Real-life Wedding belles

Malavika and Chico, Rajasthan

Bangalore residents Malavika and Chico got engaged at Nahargarh Fort outside Jaipur, where Chico grew up and still has many relatives. When the guests arrived at the venue, it was too windy to light the fire torches, so the puja and exchange of rings happened in the bright headlights of a Honda, much to car-crazy Chico's delight. Malavika fondly remembers the 'good music, delicious food, all my family and mother-in-law fussing about, the stars above and the city of Jaipur's lights twinkling below. Fireworks, too, because it was the day after Diwali.' Despite the weather, 'the dramatic result [of the stars above, the fireworks below, and the religious ceremony in the headlights of a car] was a winner,' she says.

Take me away: Destination weddings

Having your wedding in a vacation spot is a great option if you and the groom are beach bums who can't get enough of Goa, or if your wedding fantasy includes you as a Rajput princess at a fort or a palace-turned-hotel in Rajasthan. Guests love destination weddings, too. But think it through early, because having a destination wedding changes your calculations for budget, guest list, and probably date as well. Your budget might in all probability need to be expanded because the hosts of a destination wedding often pay for boarding and lodging for all guests during the festivities (though guests typically cover their own travel expenses). However, your guest list will be much smaller, as it's acceptable in this case to include only your closest family and friends, who'd truly want to travel for your affair. (Note: If all this seems like too much, you could have a destination engagement!)

Another plus point: you'll be able to get a more accurate headcount because guests usually let the host know if they're travelling in the case of a destination wedding, as costs etc. are higher. Once they take time off to be with you, they most likely won't change their plans.

Great br-ideas: Book a hotel with a branch in your city

Many hotels will let you coordinate the details for your out-of-town wedding with a representative at their hotel in your city. The sales rep can communicate with their counterpart at your destination, and provide you all the answers and details – maybe even help find you a local priest or pandit to officiate at your ceremony.

Once you have a confirmed number of guests, you might be able to negotiate a bulk price, depending on the season. And ask if they are running any promotions that might help you get more for your budget (some Goa resorts may offer a free night with your stay during the monsoon, or some destinations in Rajasthan might include a gratis safari excursion).

Hostess with the Most-ess: Your Guests

Seeing your name, together with that of your fiancé, on a beautiful wedding card that jointly invites your guests for your special day is sure to send a tingle of excitement down your spine, and make the whole thing start to feel real. But making time to greet everyone is going to be difficult—so it's best to make sure all the details are planned ahead of time!

The Indian adage 'atithi devo bhava' (the guest is God) holds especially true when your family and friends are coming from near and far to bless your wedding. You want each guest to feel special and loved—and to come away raving about your fabulous preparations, and how they had a blast. So keep the tenets of hospitality in mind as you plan—from the card you'll send out in advance asking them to block your wedding date, to the reception and/or gifts you'll have waiting when they arrive at the hotel you've arranged.

The write stuff: Wedding stationery

Your wedding card is the first introduction your guests will get to the festivities. Casual or formal, perhaps introducing colours and themes you'll repeat at the wedding, your invitation sets the mood for what's to come.

Wedding cards traditionally came in auspicious colours – which for Hindus are haldi yellow, red, and gold. Couples would adorn their names and wedding info with illustrations of a deity, a stylised Om, a set of dhol, a dancing procession, or a bride in a palki. Sikhs would opt for a shade of saffron and most likely include the khanda emblem. Muslims would select the auspicious shade of green and include the numbers 786 on the front or inside before the text of the invite; Christians traditionally selected whites or creams.

Modern brides can also try something more trendy. Classy shades of ivory, cream or off-white paper, and gold lettering are popular right now, as is heavyweight paper of 220 gsm or higher. Some printers paste together two sheets of lighter paper for a heavy effect.

The basic template is usually a card or folder that holds inserts for each function, so that brides can send some guests all of the cards, and others just the cards for the events they're invited to. Graphic designer Smita Sajnani helps her clients develop a look that reflects the bride's and groom's personalities by weaving a central concept into each set of cards. This theme could be a colour (faves are red, orange and ivory), motif (paisley or flower motifs for a modern look while religious symbols like Om are used more traditionally), or even, in one case, evocative quotes about love and the coming together of the couple.

Brides can choose between Indian-made or imported paper depending on their budgets, says Ashok Sharma, owner of Ashoka Cards, whose thirty-year-old Delhi printing company offers readymade card designs that incorporate the latest ideas in wedding stationery. Hot trends right now include paper with metallic finish, laser printing, laser cutting, as well as adding tassels and crystals to wedding cards (a trend that began a few years ago). Sharma advises, 'A combination of screen printing and foil printing with offset [printing] for the actual text can give spectacular results.' Another recent fad, according to Delhi printer Ruchika Mehta, is for couples to send their invitations in a plain outer envelope, which holds an inner envelope decorated in fancy ink, religious motifs, and the couple's names and wedding date on the outer flap of the envelope.

In addition to the bride's invitations, the groom's side usually has a different set of wedding cards for their guests. While the mother of the groom usually handles the stationery, men who are getting involved in wedding planning are increasingly also taking an interest in selecting the stationery for their side. It's common for the bride's and groom's families to approach the same printer to get their stationery coordinated.

Printers and stationery designers

Fashion-savvy belle that you are, you know your prêt from your couture. The choices are similar when it comes to wedding stationery — you can either buy off the rack from a printer, or splurge on something custom-made. (Check out our guide on pp 216-18.)

Thank you cards, programmes and more

Wedding cards may not be the only stationery you'll need for your wedding. You'll probably want to make additional cards to thank your guests for travelling to celebrate with you and bringing you gifts, whether you pre-print your thank you message, or decorate a card you can later write a personal message on. (For more on thank you notes see pp 245-48.) Some brides also make a programme that explains rituals and events – a great touch if your guests don't follow your religion and may not otherwise understand what's happening. These days, young couples often have non-Indian friends coming from abroad, who would appreciate a cheat sheet to help them through their first Indian wedding.

Whatever stationery you choose, plan ahead and buy it all together – this will allow you to coordinate the designs, and even negotiate a discount.

Great br-ideas: Invitations with personality

As we asked brides about their invitations, we noticed many of them were using non-traditional formats and materials.

Latha and Bobin, two Mumbai journalists with a sharp eye for aesthetics, commissioned good friend and designer Namrata Chattaraj to do their cards when they decided to get hitched, because she understood their taste. Together they came up with a card with a matchstick stuck on it, displaying the words: 'We found ours'. The inside was simple, with casual words outlining the venues and the dates. 'It was contemporary and quirky – just our taste,' says Latha.

Another clever Mumbai couple, Sasha and Prashant made a poster instead of a traditional wedding card. They describe themselves as opinionated, argumentative, and passionate; their caricatures were dressed in boxing outfits with gloves and standing in a boxing ring. The heading: 'A Glove Story.'

Nazia from Bangalore let her invitations say something about her and her fiancé Yassir by hiring the Belaku Trust, a rural women's NGO, to make the paper and do the paisley block printing. Nazia worked with the head of the NGO (who was also a friend) to design a mehendi insert in mustard handmade paper with a red block print motif and a nikah (wedding) insert in red with gold block printing. They bound the two cards on the side with a strip of bamboo. Working with the Belaku Trust ensured Nazia a unique card which was eco- and socio-friendly, and earned the NGO revenue and publicity.

Real-life Wedding Belles

Preeti and Kunal, 23 January , 2007, New Delhi

Preeti and Kunal both believe in a strong first impression. Preeti before marriage worked in public relations for the Grand Hotel and Kunal with his family's interiors business. So it was only fitting that their traditional, elaborate wedding – 'a grand wedding to be precise,' says Preeti – begin with the wedding stationery.

For her side, she chose a folder covered in deep red raw silk with a beautiful dabka embroidery circular motif on top in gold, green and copper. Inside was a picture from their engagement and a poem adapted from her parents, declaring their little girl grown up and ready for marriage. A stylised corner pocket held three loose gold cards for the mehendi, sangeet and wedding. The whole package was inside a dull bronze envelope with a stylised Ganeshaa line drawing and the couple's names, and was in a plain outer envelope.

Kunal's side chose a different but design-coordinated cream and gold square folder, with kundan-style embroidery and a diagonally placed ribbon inside holding cards for the mata ki chowki, mehendi, wedding, and reception. Both sides hand-delivered each of the 400 invites. Preeti's guests also received a box shaped like the card, full of kaju burfi, shakarpara, and cake. Kunal's family sent cash gifts to their relatives.

'I am glad I did not compromise; it was the first impression people had of my vision of the grand wedding I wanted, and I was very happy with the result,' declared a radiant Preeti, almost a year after her wedding. 'Most people who got my card and the accompanying box of sweets are still using the box for something or the other. Nobody threw it away,' she smiled.

Inviting your guests

In most Hindu families, the first invitation and traditional sweets are for a guest who won't personally be attending the wedding – the family deity in the temple. One Ganeshaa temple in Sawai Madhopur receives hundreds of thousands of wedding invites each wedding season, many given in person by a family member delivering the wedding card, sweets for the temple, and cash gifts; others mailed in, with token cash gifts inside.

Other religious groups have similar traditions to ensure an auspicious beginning, invoke a divine blessing, and show humility. Elders in each family usually provide guidance about where to send the first wedding card. Muslims deliver a card to their mosque before taking one to the groom's family.

We recommend sending out your cards three to six weeks before the wedding, and alerting any out-of-town guests prior to that with a 'Save the date' announcement so they'll have ample time to make their travel arrangements. Depending on family traditions and time constraints, you can hand-deliver invitations to close family and friends, and then send the rest by post. If you use a courier, be sure to ask for delivery confirmation. You may also want to call to follow up with some guests to make the invite even more personal.

Traditionally, the groom's invitations went out with a box of sweets or a token gift. This tradition has expanded to both sides now often delivering gifts with the invites. Brides and their families might send out the invites with a box of chocolates. More creative options include a silver coin memento, crystal showpiece, or porcelain figurine.

Ask the experts: Etiquette Consultant Rukshana Eisha

Is it okay for brides to invite guests via email or a website?

In my opinion, it is never a good idea to invite people over email or a website. A handwritten invitation is always a better option. For long distance guests, an email is fine, but should be followed up with a paper card.

Cyber shaadi: Wedding websites

With the internet having become the easiest and most popular way to spread information these days, many couples are setting up a personal wedding website to share the details of their wedding with friends and family. What goes on your wedding website? Practical information for your guests like the dates, times, and locations of your wedding events, plus details for out-of-towners like itineraries, accommodation, extra events and tips for shopping and sightseeing while they're in town. And then there's the fun stuff—the story of how the bride and groom met, photographs and videos of your early years and lives together, pictures and bios of families, a trivia quiz about the happy couple—the sky's the limit.

Visit ConnectedWeddings.com to set up a free wedding website.

A red carpet welcome: Hosting out-of-town guests

Traditionally, the bride's side hosts the guests who don't live locally. Though the groom's family or the couple might help with the expenses for a modern wedding, it's still customary for the hosts to treat the guests. 'All arrangements for them should be worked out in advance so that they do not have to deal with anything in a strange city,' Rukshana Eisha says.

First you'll need to figure out who's coming. Most of your out-of-town guests will hopefully let you know their arrival details and how many days they'll be staying. You and your fiancé may need to contact some of the late RSVPers by phone or email to find out if they'll be needing rooms.

Not so long ago, the bride's friends and relatives hosted out-of-town guests in their homes. This is still a great option, though is less often possible because of smaller city homes and busy lifestyles.

Real-life Wedding Belles on How They Hosted Guests

'For outstation guests we had several guides assigned to each accommodation. These guides were friends who volunteered to look after the guests, take them shopping, out to eat, and pick them up with the luxury bus to take them to all of the events. We provided luxury buses as transportation to the functions, but if they wanted to go elsewhere, we provided them with the number of a reliable car service they could call.' – Nethra, Bangalore

'My father handled guest accommodation. We did three groups — VIPs and family of the groom; friends of the bride and the groom; other important guests — and then selected first-class, medium and budget hotel rooms. As we were in a small town, the wedding planners rented houses for a week. I would say that it is best not to have anybody stay in your house, even if you have spare bedrooms. The day before the wedding you don't want any bickering or issues. It should just be you and your family.' – Latha, Mumbai

So, depending on the number of rooms you need and your budget, check out hotels, service apartment or house rentals, private clubs (like the India International Centre and the India Habitat Centre in Delhi; CCI, Radio Club, Willingdon and Gymkhana in Mumbai; the Bangalore Club and the Bowring Institute in Bangalore), guest houses, company accommodation (if your company provides, or a friend's company does), or dormitory-style housing (for younger friends).

If you have family member in the armed forces, you may be able to rent rooms for a good rate at one of the armed forces mess facilities though prices vary depending on how close a relative recommends your case, and some facilities are limited to only immediate family. Travel agents and wedding planners are good sources for help.

Harshe Gupta, Director of Sardana Events and Entertainment, recommends renting farm houses when putting up guests in Delhi. 'As an added advantage you can even have some of the smaller wedding-related events there itself, making it easier for the guests to get to events,' Gupta says. Gupta also advises hiring buses for transferring guests to the wedding venue so you can manage your group all at once – plus a few cars/taxis just in case somebody needs to go home earlier than the group or is left behind inadvertently.

Putting your guests up at a five-star hotel also has perks, if you can fit it into your budget, since top properties offer high quality amenities and go out of their way to accommodate large groups. For example, the Taj Palace Hotel in New Delhi offers wedding party groups a block of rooms in the same area of the hotel; complimentary breakfast at a private banquet venue; chocolates, fresh flowers and exotic fruits in every room; dessert and cognac brought to the room at the time of turndown service; a separate hospitality desk; and discounts on laundry service.

Every great hostess greets her guests with a warm welcome. Have a friend or relative meet them at the airport or train station to bring them to their hotel. Give them a printed itinerary with the pick-up and drop-off timings and venues for wedding events and additional meals, if applicable, and information about shopping and sightseeing. The more detail, the better, so guests understand which meals you'll be hosting. (If you're worried guests will bill room service or other hotel charges to the room that you're not prepared to pay for, you can add a tactful request to your note asking them to refrain from doing so, or diplomatically spell out that only the room tariff has been paid in advance.) It's also crucial to include the mobile number of a contact person. You'll be very busy as the bride, so ask your mother, father, sibling, uncle or wedding planner if they mind being main contact on call.

You know the wedding events calendar best, so try to anticipate what your guests might need to be comfortable during their stay. The women might appreciate help coordinating ironing for their formalwear and trips to the beauty parlour. If you have guests from overseas, they'd probably love some background on the events and help shopping for appropriate attire. If possible, ask a friend or family member to meet guests at the hotel to help coordinate transportation to meals or events – even to help shop for that elusive sari, at the most American-friendly showroom, that will best complement your blonde college classmate's complexion.

You could even arrange a short tour around your city, of the local sights. Or if there's a free day between your mehendi and the wedding day, or after the wedding, organise a day trip: Agra if in Delhi, Mysore if in Bangalore, Lonavala or Madh Island, if in Mumbai.

Great br-ideas: Gifts

Leave a welcome basket waiting in your guests' hotel rooms, with snacks and bottles of water. Or thank them at the end of their stay with a box of sweets before everybody says goodbye, or a CD of photographs from the ceremonies. (You could also send pictures in the mail with your thank you note later.)

Getting the Wedding Belle Look

Your wedding day is one you've secretly (or not so secretly) looked forward to ever since Barbie met Ken. And even after you grew out of the pink plastic phase, you know the importance of attractive packaging. You and your own hero may talk about things on a higher plane — souls entwining and hearts soaring — but you know that the here and now is important, too. You don't want to look back to your wedding pictures and lament a bad hair day, blotchy skin or a wardrobe fatality. Even the most modest woman wants to look her very best on her wedding day.

But don't let the pressure get to you. It's okay if you're not able to channel your inner Monica from *Friends*, who had everything planned to a T, complete with a wedding book filled with satin swatches. We've got your back, your front, and your accessories. Here's all you need to do to present the most glamorous version of yourself on your wedding day.

Wedding traditions

According to a Gujarati custom, on the arrival of the baraat, the bride's mother playfully tries to catch the groom's nose between her thumb and forefinger, as one might do with a naughty child, to remind him that he is taking away her daughter and is now responsible for her happiness.

Bride style quiz: Identify your look

Each bride brings her own brand of charm to her wedding. But as unique as each girl's preparations for her wedding can be, there are certain basic elements in her mental make-up that indicate what kind of bridal avatar she will flaunt. Take our Bride Style Quiz to determine what kind of bride you'll be.

Your idea of fun is:
a) An afternoon at home with family
b) Cappuccino with your girlfriends
c) Sophisticated dinner and drinks with your clique
d) Paintball with your buddies

To relax, you listen to:
a) Golden oldies
b) The latest pop songs
c) Indian or Western classical, opera
d) World music

Your favourite accessory is:
a) The gold pendant your parents gave you for your 16th birthday
b) Jewelled hair clips
c) Diamonds, dahling
d) Your navel ring

Your dream destination is:
a) Anywhere where you can catch up with relatives and visit places of worship
b) Anywhere where you can see the sights and get a little shopping in, too
c) Anywhere you can shop for premium brands
d) Anywhere off the map

Mostly a: You're the traditional type, the genuine gharelu bahu that your in-laws will love. Tussars and Benarasi saris in traditional red and maroon suit you best. For a bit of adventure on the less formal occasions, try rust and emerald. Wear only designs that you're comfortable in. Don't let the hoardings on every street that show dare-to-bare brides pressure you into something less modest than you're used to.

Mostly b: Girlie as a girl can get, your feminine charms can only be enhanced by pinks and purples. This is a day that seems tailor-made for you; you can act all demure and ladylike, just like you love to. But you're quite clued in to what looks good on you. You know you can carry off chiffon and chanderi with equal élan. Go for sweetheart necklines and puff sleeves for blouses.

Mostly c: Personable and with it, your girlfriends have always considered you the go-to girl for glam. Now that it's your turn to shine in the shaadi spotlight, you can pull out all the stops. Get the designer lehenga and the vintage jewels. Aubergine with amethyst, hot pink with rose quartz and rubies, ice blue with diamonds... And thanks to your gym-going and body-worshipping ways, you're usually the bride who can wear the tiny choli and the midriff-baring lehenga without looking risque or worse—tawdry.

Mostly d: Is there anything you won't try?!! Experimental and adventurous, you're the sort of gal who'd wear her beloved boots with her bandhani silk. Why not use that free-spirited enthusiasm for eclectic style to pair your grandma's French lace with a sexy, faux leather halter for the cocktail? Or use your magic touch to fuse unlikely shades such as fuchsia and lemon, or wine and dove grey? Just keep in mind that many of your relatives and in-laws may not understand your sense of style. But, of course, that's never really bothered you, has it?

A Year's Worth of Goodies: Your Trousseau

There now, once that's done you have the broad outlines under which you can go forth and SHOP! For most of us, this is one of the most exciting parts of the process of getting married. When else in life do you have a budget larger than ever before and people encouraging you to pick up prettier and prettier outfits? Let's start with the trousseau!

The trousseau comprises all the things you'll need for your new life in your new home. Have you been laying away for this since you were ten or is this going to be a stupendous store crawl? From a few choice ensembles to entire new wardrobes; a dinner set to a modular kitchen—how each bride chooses her trousseau varies vastly in terms of tastes, traditions, time, and finances. However you do it, it's fun to imagine enjoying each selection with your new hubby.

In some communities, it's customary to display the trousseau at some pre-wedding functions (like the sangeet). In this case, your family may want to showcase more showy items, symbolic of status. Montessori teacher Mamta from Mumbai, who had her trousseau professionally packed and displayed at her reception, says, 'It's traditional to do it, but I didn't even choose my own things. I haven't worn any of the heavy gold jewellery and the richly embellished saris since, nor used the silver plates. But my parents and in-laws were so visibly happy doing this that I didn't interfere.'

Homemaker Rumana from Surat also remembers how her family insisted she have four really heavy jewellery sets made. 'These don't quite work with any of the casual salwar-kameez that I generally wear. But apart from them, the things I chose were perfect. I had ten formal salwar kameez sets and ten casual ones tailored. I bought make-up, lingerie, sleepwear, and even my favourite shampoo and conditioner in large quantities! It's not like I can't buy all that later, but it helps to have your own stock of essentials for the first few months so that you don't have to go through the awkwardness of asking for them while you're still getting to know everyone. Especially so if you're not financially independent and your marriage is an arranged one like mine was.'

So how does a bride amass all this stuff? The traditional way is to start collecting years in advance. Women used to sew and embroider clothes and linen for years. Today, you might just need to visit a superstore to check off the following.

Clothes: Traditional or Western casuals and formals, loungewear, exercise gear, lingerie and sleepwear (practical and romantic), swimwear, workwear, partywear, etc. Basically, all that will see you through your pre-wedding functions, wedding, reception, honeymoon and first few months as newly-weds. Depending on how appropriate it is (how accepting of your tattered old nightie or silver miniskirt will the denizens of your new home be?), decide to keep some of your wardrobe, or buy a whole new one.

Personal essentials: All the gadgets, hygiene products, lotions and potions that you use. Everything from soap, mouthwash, shampoo, conditioner, and moisturiser, to hair serum, face and body scrubs and packs, deodorants, per-fumes as well as make-up and peripherals like brushes, blow-dryers, straighteners, curlers, hairclips and epilators, etc.

Accessories: Jewellery of all styles and values, clips, belts, scarves, sunglasses, handbags and footwear of all kinds.

Linen: Bed and bath linen needn't be part of your trousseau, but is often included.

Kitchen and home accessories: From pressure cookers and casseroles to microwave ovens and plasma TVs, what goes into your shopping bag depends on what you need and what you can afford. Try to drop hints to some of your guests if there's a particular espresso machine or ice-cream maker you've got your eye on! (Or put them on your wish-list, if you're circulating one.) Of course, you'll need less of these if you and your fiancé are moving into his family home.

When setting the trousseau budget keep the following factors in mind:

- Your total wedding budget. A realistic one that falls somewhere between the thriftiest budget you've conscientiously put together in your head and the extravagant one of your dreams, that gives your dad nightmares. (See our information about budgeting on pp 31–45)
- Complete clarity on who will be spending on what. Traditionally, the bride's family spends on most of the wedding functions except for the reception (which is on the groom's side). But in modern weddings, the costs are often borne equally.
- What level of priority you want to give to the trousseau within this budget. As a modern-day bride, you might not really prepare a trousseau at all, preferring to shift all your existing possessions to your new home. You might be working and living on your own, or with friends, independent of your parents, with much of what you'll need. Importantly, you then go towards bridal finery, the honeymoon and life after the wedding.
- Where you're shopping. Prices vary from city to city and even area to area. If you have some time, you could work out a plan that allows for you to shop around within your city for competitive prices and deals, or even go further away from your turf for better deals.
- A realistic idea of what your life after marriage is going to be like. If you're going to be largely homebound in a smaller town, you'd want to spend more on padding your nest rather than on dressy clothes that you may not have the opportunity to wear. Consider weather conditions, your in-laws' sensibilities if you're living with them, etc. When Chanelle was preparing for her new life with husband-to-be Chris in Toronto, Canada, she planned ahead. 'Since I was going to be joining him abroad less than a month after we were married in Hyderabad, he very wisely suggested that my family and I not invest in heavy saris or jewellery. Instead, we concentrated on getting clothes to suit the style and temperature there,' recalls Chanelle.
- Styles change. So there's no point buying five pairs of modish leggings which will go out of style in a couple of weeks. Think classic and long term: the simple white kurta, the solid-colour cuffed shirt, the traditional silk sari. You can update with accessories later.

Dress-perate? Don't be: How to plan your wedding outfits

Even if you've chosen a big fat Indian wedding and you're on a budget or strapped for time, don't be daunted. While the wedding and reception call for the most expensive and beautiful outfits you can dream up, you can go less elaborate for smaller functions. You want to be able to enjoy your own wedding, so opt for clothing that's easy to move around in. Today, the embellishment (embroidery, sequins, Swarovski crystals, lace, net, etc.) of outfits for the engagement, mehendi or cocktail party can be minimal, as long as the overall look is plush and pretty.

Some broad guidelines to get you started:

Engagement: Elegant and understated. A sari works best for this, in beautiful yet classy colours. Try hues that are traditional yet light; peach, pink, aqua, pale yellow are all good options. A silk sari with a thin gold border works very well too.

Sangeet: Choose something ornate yet fun, which will allow you the freedom to get up and do your version of '*Mere haathon mein nao nao choodiyan*'! A lehenga or sharara is good for this event, with light detailing and work. Hot colours: mint, fuchsia, sunflower, aubergine, orange and funky combinations of these and other striking ones like deep red, cobalt or mustard.

Mehendi: Traditional and graceful, simple and elegant, preferably in a shade of green or maroon. Keep in mind that you'll have to sit for what will seem like hours while your bridal mehendi is being applied, so your outfit should be comfortable, unfussy, and mishap-proof, in a colour and pattern that takes into account the messiness of mehendi.

Cocktails: An Indian ensemble (but more fitted than usual as this is one of the more modern, sophisticated events—as opposed to the formal, traditional engagement, or main event), a Western gown or a fusion of the two (for example, a corset top over a flowy skirt with a matching stole wrapped around your shoulders), is appropriate for this night. Warning: If your cocktails are going to include narrow-minded relatives from out of town who won't understand that your revealing little black dress can be just as elegant as a silk bandgala, go for the latter. You want to be remembered for all the right reasons, right?

Various religious functions and family gatherings: Go with saris or salwar-kameez sets for these—both flattering and sober enough to have them all fawning over the bahu-to-be.
Religious ceremony: Preferably something very traditional, opulent, and demure. Love those period pieces, and always wanted to be Parineeta or Paro? You could go with a vintage wedding sari (even the one your grandma got married in!), a Benarasi, Dharmavaram or Kanjeevaram silk one, or an ornate lehenga. Time to let your inner Jodhaa out!
Reception: Something bolder, such as a lehenga with a bustier or a designer sari with a backless choli. (The advantage of the latter is that you can always draw your pallu up over a scantily clad back, and let it drop when you're letting your hair down later.) The trend is to wear something glamorous, fun and Indian, with a hint of skin. But if you prefer to be the coy newly-wed, you can still rely on something classic and heavily embellished.

How much in advance should you plan your outfits?

The planning period ranges from off-the-rack in an hour for those brides rushing to the mandap, to regular, organised shopping trips, a year ahead, for the divas of detail. Archana, who married Vijay in January 2007 in Mumbai, says, 'I had started shopping for my wedding around eight months before the actual date as I didn't want to keep stuff for the last minute. Every Sunday, I'd take a friend along and just go to different sari shops, and when something caught my eye I'd just buy it. I was more than satisfied with my wedding day look. I decided on saris so that I'd be able to wear them again. Also, I'm not someone who's very comfortable in chaniya cholis or gowns, and I like to keep things simple.'

Ready-to-wear lines are up for grabs for brides who prefer to get right to it, but custom-made designer wear naturally takes much longer and is of course more expensive. According to Delhi-based fashion designer Ritu Kumar, a bridal outfit on order can take anything from three to six months to execute. She says, 'If you don't have enough time, go with something readymade or partially ready. Normally, two or three fittings are required to give a proper finish. A fitting with options of different odhnis and blouses takes anything from two to three hours.'

Our recommendation: Even if you're going for readymade outfits, start surveying the market about three months (and no less than a month) in advance. Then you'll have time to shop around, and get alterations done. Bridal fashion trends don't change as rapidly as regular trends, so a few months won't make your apparel and accessories look dated.

Buying guide

You have to decide what you prefer—each bride must choose to buy off the rack, use a family tailor and/or go the couture route. Perhaps you can spend a day visiting a bridal store, a seamstress and a designer to explore your options and see which one fits your vision and budget. This section will show you how to go through the entire process with each of these options and get the most value for your money.

Shop rite: Ready-to-vow bridalwear

Given what our country is like—with festivities and a vibrant wedding season that runs almost through the year—you'll always find sales or at least be able to leverage something for a discount. If you think you're an ace in the boardroom, wait till you meet bridalwear salespeople. On important shopping trips, bring a reasonably plump budget, your advisory committee (the fewer people the better if you've narrowed it down to one or two vendors) and, most importantly, your negotiating skills.

Great br-ideas

A trend today is for the entire bridal party to dress in a similar colour scheme or embroidery style a la K3G. For this colour-coordinated, great Indian wedding, it's especially vital to plan much in advance and in the greatest detail.

Your bridal shopping checklist

Come prepared. Have your measurements close at hand, some pictures from magazines you like and think would look good on you, as well as photographs of any jewellery you want to match (you can do this vice versa too, and pick the jewellery after the outfits).

Be confident. The customer is queen and a bride has more buying power than most others—assert yourself. Find a salesperson with a friendly face to guide you through their wares.

Shortlist and spreadsheet. Once you've explained what you want and they've shown you the options, try on those you like and shortlist. Make notes about each of them (fabric, style, marked price, pros and cons) on a spreadsheet or in your journal, depending on your planning style; see them under different light settings and ask if you can take some shots on your phone or camera for future reference. Note: Some stores may not allow this, to protect their designs.

Shop around. Visit a few stores to get an idea of what's on offer. Even if you think you absolutely love an ensemble, give yourself time. Can you visualise yourself being the glowing bride in it? Does it suit your complexion, body type, height, personality? Which function is it best suited for? Does it go with the décor/ theme you're planning?

Don't be too shy to negotiate. Once you're convinced an outfit is the right one for you, go back to the store and start negotiating. Don't let the snootiness of some salespeople intimidate you into buying anything beyond your budget—you don't need to impress them. Enjoy yourself and don't be an overbearing bridezilla. Pleasant banter usually results in 10% off or some useful bonus—a dupatta, or matching stole for the groom. (Note: Most vendors offer free alterations, unless a large portion of the embroidery has to be redone.)

Manage the people who'll help create your trousseau. In many traditional weddings, all the outfits to be worn post the kanyadaan (in a Hindu wedding), including the shaadi ka joda, are gifted by the in-laws. If this is the case, just give them your measurements and maybe preferences. Some brides-to-be go shopping with their mother-in-law or sisters-in-law; a great way to break the ice and bond. On the other hand, it could also be full of pitfalls if tastes, budgets and shopping methods clash. So, do make a few compromises. For example, if they're urging you to try something uber gaudy, be a sport and try on one or two, then find something that falls perhaps somewhere between their taste and yours. Don't become their dress-up doll, but don't dig your heels in either—you don't want to be labelled 'stubborn', a label you might have trouble losing later. Tip: Take your cronies along (mom or sis or friends) so you can call for a show of hands on that not-so-you, sherry-coloured sharara.

Look beyond yourself. You're the star at your wedding, of course. But from your best friend to your bhabhi, everyone will want to look fab at your functions—so make that extra effort to see that they're on the same page. Try shopping together for great discounts at tailors and stores, and, more importantly, increased attention and better service.

Darzis and designers: Custom-made to perfection

Family tailor: Tailor-made can sometimes be the most affordable option, since unlike in the West, bespoke tailoring doesn't necessarily cost you the earth here. If you have a family tailor who's consistently delivered up-to-the-mark garments, trusting him with your wedding look could work out cheaper than buying from an upmarket boutique or designer prêt line, and this guy knows what you like to wear. If he's a good copycat, use the many wedding catalogues and magazines on hand; it's easy to pick a pattern to duplicate. And most shops have an embroidery expert on call. The only drawback is you'll never be sure what things look like until the final fitting.

Designer couture: At the other end of the spectrum is exclusive designer wear, custom-made especially for you; colour, cut, style and trimmings. Some designers even go to the extent of dying the fabric a particular shade that's right for you. With this one-of-a-kind detailing, there's little chance of your outfit matching another bride's or worse, that one of your guests could show up in a similar glamorous ensemble! You can be assured that you'll look like a million bucks. But be prepared to possibly shell out almost as much! Depending on the designer you use and what you want made, a typical couture wedding outfit can cost from Rs 20,000 to a crore.

In both cases, you'll need to have fitting sessions. If you're looking after all the nitty-gritties of your nikah (and probably working at the same time), you may find it tough to work them into your busy bridal schedule, so do plan ahead.

Fitting in fittings

You should, ideally, have two fittings for a custom-made ensemble. Remember that you'll need to have fittings for each outfit you get stitched, so budget your time. Though if you have the same store's tailor do all (or most) of your alterations (if they have enough resources), you may be able to minimise your visits.

Alterations timeline

(To be followed for each wedding outfit. Talk to your tailor/designer as he/she may have additional ideas or requirements.)

At least 10–12 weeks before the wedding: Visit the tailor/designer. Choose fabric, embroidery, and pattern. Give measurements.

At least 6–8 weeks before the wedding: Fitting 1. At this point, the garment should be ready in its basic form. Your tailor/designer may still have to handwork some extra embellishments, but you can get an idea of the fit and fall of it and ask for whatever little changes you think are necessary. While a stand-in with similar body structure as yours could do the job (if you're absolutely tied up at work, the sister you've been sharing clothes with for ages could take your place), she may not have your vision or aesthetics, so it's better you make the time so you're not disappointed with the end result on the big day.

2 weeks before the wedding: By this time, your outfit should be 99.9 per cent ready. Fitting 2 is about last-minute adjustments only, and should be of much shorter duration than the first one. Do take along your jewellery and any other accessories to see how your final look will come together; you may want to nix that extra bit of embellishment if your jewellery's doing the work already. If you can coordinate your hair and make-up people (unless they're really high profile and only work from their salon), this is a good time for them to see your wedding outfit and decide what war paint will best work with it.

Remember:

- For a custom-made sari, the embroidery may take longer, but the stitching is only limited to the fall and the blouse, so it may be an easier and quicker option than a lehenga.

- It's important that you take into account any diet regime you're following and share your targets (realistic ones) with the person taking measurements. Redoing embroidery is expensive. So, if you're doing an ab workout that you think will reduce a few inches off your tummy, it's better to get the heaviest embroidery done below hip level; this way there's leeway for alterations at the waist. For the same reason, if you're toning up your arms, avoid intricate embellishment on your sleeves.
- Don't schedule your last fitting for just a few days before the wedding—leave yourself (and your tailor) time for an extra nip and tuck just in case something is amiss, or if you lose more weight than intended (which often happens to brides because of all the stress and excitement).

Wardrobe function: Storage

Okay, you've got your beautiful bridal finery right on time (with a week to spare). Good show. But now you're wondering how to store it all so the outfits will be creaseless, spotless and fresh for the big day. If you're strapped for space in your wardrobe, put all the casual wear and other clothes that you know you won't need for another few weeks into suitcases and heave them up into your storage area. Empty your cupboard's hanging space completely. Wipe it clean and scatter a few sachets of lavender or rose before you hang up your treasures. Where possible, hang them without any folding, so that you won't need to risk an iron on them on the final day. Ensure there are no damp spots, insects or things that can stain or rip the delicate clothes.

Great br-ideas: Fitting in pre-fitting shopping

To really think ahead, purchase the appropriate lingerie and footwear for each outfit before you go for your first fitting, so your tailor can work your bra lines and heel height into his plans.

Ask the experts: Ritu Kumar recommends

The beloved Delhi-based designer gave us her take on what's coming up on the horizon of bridal fashion.

Upcoming trends

* Bridal lines are getting more interesting by way of colour and embellishment.

* In 2008–09, we will see a lot more metallic surfaces, like work with gota and patti kaa kaam.

* But the bridal look remains traditional, glamorous, and rich. Plush, classical colours are always in. A wave towards burgundy with heavy embellishments is evident.

* Pastels will also make a comeback, especially for morning weddings.

* Cholis are getting experimental and a lot more will happen on this front, such as low backs or half sleeves with reverse embellishments to the lehengas or saris.

Ritu recommends some sure-fire ways to stand out stylishly

* If you're a more experimental bride, opt for a rich but glamorous silhouette, which is fitted at the top of the lehenga, but flares out at the bottom.

* Contrasted colours of cholis, with a deep neck and a tie-up back can look interesting.

* You can add spunk to lehengas and odhnis by using different colour palettes for each. For instance, a gold and red lehenga with an olive green blouse and a red and olive odhni can be fun.

* A see-through, net dupatta, with just a hint of glitter, gives a lighter look. Or you could try a soft peach or coral lehenga with silver embroidery and highlight it with diamond jewellery.

Best foot forward: Bridal footwear

- The length of your sari or ghagra will depend on how high your heels are.
- Make the final buy after you choose your outfits so you can match colours and textures.
- If there's one gold or silver pair that's perfect, wear it for more than one wedding event.
- Buy from a reliable store, preferably somewhere you've been shopping for a while.
- Break in a new pair; wear them around the house, scuff the bottoms so you wont slip.
- Anticipate trouble by using pads or gel inserts to make your pair more comfy. No pair of shoes leaves you pain free after extended wear through a wedding day. Footwear isn't in the spotlight as much as your face is, so a shoe that makes you grimace just won't do.

Ask the experts: Footwear designer Rina Shah

The popular owner of the boutique Rinaldi offers her advice on footwear fashion.

Bridal footwear trends in 2008–09 and beyond:

Bridal trends are still going to feature a lot of bling with stones, Swarovski crystals and semi-precious stone work. Heels will be high, but comfort is very important. Copper and a dull antique look with stones like kundan will be most in demand.

What's so special about custom-made shoes?

A custom pair is made to fit perfectly, being custom measured to your foot. Making the shoes takes between 2 and 15 days, depending on the style and the amount of work on the shoes. This can vary from precious stones to all kinds of embroidery, and all kinds of materials as well as beading etc. Custom shoes are one of a kind, and vary from between Rs 3,500 and Rs 10,500.

Buying tips

Brides should match their shoes with the gold or silver jewellery they are going to wear. This makes more sense than matching them with your clothing, as this may restrict you from wearing them again. But generally, most bridal footwear matches the outfit, often in red, bronze, gold, pink, etc.

Inner pieces: Lingerie

For some reason, moms and older sisters think your wedding gives them carte blanche to encourage you to do away with those three packs of granny-style cotton panties. Friends, too, get into the act with gusto. Graphic designer Puja from Pune, who got married in June 2006, is still embarrassed by the memory of the edible undies her gal pals gifted her at her hen party. 'I'm not a prude as such, but it was a gruelling experience explaining to my folks at home what those frightful pink things that looked like a cross between candy floss and Ugly Betty's underpants were! I wouldn't be caught dead wearing something that awful on my honeymoon anyway.'

Well, like Puja, you may not be too game for adventure or wackiness. However, you can have fun with your options. If you think buying off the rack at Marks and Spencer instead of the neighbourhood hosiery store is the full extent of your choice, think again. Brands like Aubade, Boudoir London, Etam, Enamour, La Senza, La Perla, Lovable, Triumph and many more, have bold and beautiful bridal lines, with satin, lace and velvet. Indian brides are getting increasingly adventurous with their andar wear.

What lies beneath: You don't want to feel your strap slip or snap, or the underwire dig into your ribs while you take the pheras. And when you and the mister are greeting guests on the reception dais, the last thing you want on your mind is whether you're spilling out of that skimpy choli. Delish delicates give you the right support and silhouette. From bras and panties, to petticoats (to be worn under saris) and slips (for under a flimsy lehenga if required), everything should be colour coordinated, whenever possible. Maybe have cups sewn in, or use a transparent-strap bra. Neutrals which stand out from the colour of your outfit are an absolute no-no; nothing's tackier than an out-of-place strap.

Marketing professional Neha asked her friend in the US for lingerie from Victoria's Secret for her February 2007 wedding, 'I wore lingerie the same colour as my rose pink lehenga.' For her other ensembles, her blouses were padded.

When it all comes off: You want to look fabulous on your wedding night and honeymoon, whether you're the blushing touch-me-not or the 'let's get it on, lover boy' sort. Now that top international lingerie brands are for sale in India—from La Perla vintage corsets, to Dolce and Gabbana rose-print camisoles and boy-leg briefs, to silk pyjama sets from Fredericks of Hollywood—it's tough to decide. Pretty pastels or frisky fuchsia? Lace or lycra? Sheer or satiny? Even tried-and-tested labels like Victoria's Secret and Wonderbra seem commonplace, when you think of unusual finds from labels like Agent Provocateur or Spank (short for Sexy Panties And Naughty Knickers) you can find on the black market or order from abroad. Bling bikinis for that honeymoon in Baga or Bali, and sexy sleepwear that suits your new Smugly Married status, are essentials too.

What's trendy now: The latest in lingerie

The girlie look—naughty yet romantic, rather than last season's raunchy and racy—is very hot right now. Corsets and camisoles with interesting trim and detailing, especially in champagne-coloured satin, which suits most Indian skin tones. Feminine touches like frills, polka dots or pretty florals, while the colour palette goes from cream to delicate old rose to vibrant and vivacious sherbet and jewel tones like turquoise, fuchsia, purple and jade, apart from dove and baby pink, animal prints and kohl black. The most desirable fabrics range from organic Austrian cotton to sensuous silk, satin and velvet, ruffled chiffon, sheer tulle. Add-ons like lace, tie-ups, rosebuds, bows, leather detailing, sequins, diamantes, tassels, faux fur or feather trim up the fun factor. But do remember there's a time and place for everything, even lacy lingerie!

Shopping tips

Measure your bra size

Bra size isn't going to come to you through divine intervention. All it takes is a tape measure and some simple maths. Or a visit to a special sizing salon like Debenhams in Delhi or Boudoir London in Mumbai. Don't be embarrassed or shocked if you realise you've been wearing the wrong size all of your grown-up life. Many others are in the same situation.

Bra sizing consists of a band size and a cup size, which is why sizes come in a pair of a number and a letter, like 34A or 36D.

Step 1, measuring band size: Measure around the ribcage, directly under the bust, so that the tape measure rests on the lower band of your bra. The tape should be smooth across the back and fit snugly. Add 5 to this measurement to obtain your band or chest size. For example, if your ribcage measurement is 31" + (5) = 36" band size. If the resulting measurement plus 5 is an odd number like 33", you can usually go to the next even band size (34"), but you may also want to try the next lower one (32").

Step 2, measuring cup size: Measure completely around the bust at its fullest point. The difference between this measurement and your band size is your cup size. Each inch of difference is equal to one cup size. For example, if your band size is 36" and your bust measurement 37", you're an A cup. If the difference is less than 1 inch, AA cup; 1" = A cup; 2" = B cup; 3" = C cup; 4" = D cup; 5" = DD cup.

The basics

* Get a few whites, blacks and neutrals with good support, which take you through the long flights, sightseeing and adventure sports on your honeymoon.

* A few simple yet pretty options for that relaxed lunch or romantic evening.

* A couple of really sexy stunners with whatever floats your boat (and hopefully his!) as embellishment—French lace, Swarovski, feathers, diamantes, sequins, frills, cut-outs, saucy messages, etc. If you haven't known him long enough to know what turns him on or off, play it a little safer with elegant satin or lace ensembles; not remotely kinky. And jewel tones and pristine pastels, good for any skin tone. Keep the sleepwear simple; sensuous baby dolls and barely-there negligees.

Get a good deal

- Most big brands have sales at regular intervals and some have customer loyalty programmes. Track sale dates and make sure you get there early to get the most variety. If you missed the sales, use loyalty programme points you've earned on previous purchases.
- If a brand has multiple outlets, visit to get more options on colours and styles.
- Keep your eyes and ears open for sales way in advance, start stockpiling your arsenal.
- Suss out multiple brand sales in five-star hotels—you'll get discounted foreign brands.
- Scour the export outlets — but be vigilant and inspect what you buy.
- If you or people you know are travelling abroad during the sale season, you can always ask them to get you specific pieces you choose from online stores.

Get in on the secret

Get familiar with these lingerie wonders to ask for when you shop:

Transparent straps: These plastic wonders are on almost every second shoulder these days, their sheer presence going well with spaghetti straps or off-shoulder corsets. Many stores sell an extra pair to substitute for your original straps.

Nipple covers: Round or petal-shaped stickers that help cover your nipples in cold weather or embarrassing situations when wearing a body-hugging top sans bra.

Body tape: Double-sided sticky tape that keeps slippery low-cut party tops and dresses from revealing more than necessary. Famously used by Jennifer Lopez and other Hollywood stars to keep garments in place.

Body-shapers: Girdle-type bottoms that suck in your tummy and butt, made of strong elastic fabric—à la the famous granny underpants of Bridget Jones. These are great as they help give your body a more controlled silhouette, even if you may not be ready to model them for your new hubby—at least for a while!

Gel pads: Squidgy yet safe inserts that you can put into your bra. An easy way to plump up your bustline so an outfit fits better.

Get the vocab

The world of innerwear has its own lingerie lexicon. Get familiar with the terminology and you'll get what you want in half the time!

Baby doll: A tiny A-line satin or lace camisole with a high waist that's worn under a dressing gown on those honeymoon mornings when you never want to get out of the hotel room.

Balconette bra: A shelf-like brassiere that uplifts without covering the chest completely, to emphasise cleavage. Great for that beautiful choli or the low-cut little black designer dress at the cocktail.

Boy brief: The legs extend to the top of the thigh, while the waistband sits on the hips, providing full coverage of the back. Usually seamed in front and back, gives a smooth line from waist to hip. A nice change on that romantic yet relaxed holiday.

Bustier: A short, tight-fitting, strapless bodice that can be embellished and worn as a sari blouse for a less formal occasion or under a jacket for a Western-style party. Choose a pretty colour or one that will match everything; red or fuchsia, or good old black or white.

Camisole: A sleeveless undergarment in delicate fabric with thin straps. A good honeymoon option: glam up your bedroom look or pair with a sexy pencil skirt for a night on the town.

Contour bra: Padded or lined cups and underwire (see below) help impart a smooth shape and eliminate nipple visibility. Perfect under T-shirts, chiffon or flimsy garments, in a nude or matching hue.

Convertible/Strapless bra: Straps may be detached, can also be worn conventionally, criss-crossed at the back or like a halter (see below). Helps when your outfit has an unusual neckline or sleeves.

Corset: Close-fitting, often with boning and lace-ups for additional support and streamlining body contours. Can be worn with a sari or skirt. Designers from

Manish Arora to Rocky S have all added their creativity to these; traditionally worn under dresses for a slimmer silhouette, but now a fashion statement on their own.

Demi-cup: A low-cut bra that enhances cleavage, especially if cups are fully padded. Adds definition for those dare-to-bare cholis.

Fishnets: These are very 1980s-style stockings in criss-cross material. Wear with a garter and belt if you want to go the whole hog.

G-string: A thong with no back coverage, as the strip at the back is even thinner than in a thong. Your little surprise for him!

Halter: Straps go behind the neck and are hidden when you're wearing a blouse with a halter neck, in-cut sleeves or a deep neckline.

Negligee: A wisp of a nightie with thin straps on the shoulders and a straight or A-line cut, made in lace, satin, georgette or even the softest, sheerest mulmul, covers you from chest to mid-thigh.

Padded bra: Padded lower cups, works well for a fuller bustline. Also, it makes outfits fall better on some smaller-busted women.

Push-up bra: Padded inside cups, creates a fuller look and enhances cleavage for those ensembles that need all the support they can get.

Seamless bra: Does not have seam stitching on the cups, thus creating a smooth appearance that works fabulously under tees and tank tops (similar to a contour bra, but this one doesn't add definition).

Teddy: A camisole and panty combined in one piece. Fitted to the body or loose, worn under clothing or as seductive sleepwear.

Thong: A panty thats high cut on the leg with a thin strip at the back that eliminates panty lines. Perfect under pants or thin Indian wear.

Underwire bra: Semicircular wire supports are sewn into the underside of cups to give better definition and support to the breasts. Most bras today are underwired.

Sets and sensibility: Jewellery

The essentials

Desi weddings and jewellery are inextricably linked. No wedding is complete without the basic jewellery that accompanies the rites, and 22-karat gold's the traditional way to go.

Even the most modest wedding will have the bride's parents giving her a gold ring, a gold necklace with matching earrings and at least half a dozen gold bangles. The bride wears these at the wedding. She wears a similar set, gifted by the groom's family, at the reception or the bidai (taking leave) ceremony. Importantly, the black bead and gold mangalsutra that the groom puts around his new wife's neck is a sacred symbol of their marriage bond, like wedding rings in the West, and is universal among Hindus across the country. Apart from these, there are all sorts of traditional jewellery pieces that feature in wedding ceremonies across India. We've included a few examples:

- In parts of north India, silver anklets and bichhuas (toe rings) are part of the package.
- In parts of the south, a nose ring or two and a gold thaali pendant proclaim your married status—the latter is in effect the mangalsutra.
- Punjabi brides have a set of 21 white and red bangles called a chooda, which is given by the maternal uncle on the morning of the wedding and worn for six weeks to a year.
- For Muslims, there's no specific wedding jewellery, but some brides wear a crescent-shaped hair ornament on the side of their head, a nose ring and glass bangles, gifts from the groom's family. Heavy jewellery has become part of the wedding finery here too.
- Sikh brides wear a gold-coin necklace called a mohra, as well as the Punjabi chooda.
- The primary adornment of Parsi and Christian brides may be the wedding rings and the beautiful attire (white madhavate sari and Western-style white gown or Kerala sari on some pre-wedding occasions, respectively), but today, they vie with their Hindu counterparts in sporting bountiful wedding baubles. In Kerala, of course, a bride's gold collection can compete with north Indian gold collections.

What's right for you

Clearly, wedding jewellery varies from community to community and region to region. The best way for you to find out what's suitable for you is to consult knowledgeable family members and/or use the internet. But if you want to go really ethnic and be close to your roots when you're tying the knot, spend an afternoon with some of your community elders. Even if you don't have close relations who are in the know, there are enough elderly women in every community who would love a young bride to consult them. Who knows, one of them may even offer to loan you an antique piece or two!

If yours is a mixed marriage, then you can blend the best of both worlds and pick and choose from both sets of customs. What you wear will also depend on personal choice. And whereas the old concept—that the more gold and diamonds a bride wore, the higher the status of her parents—may still be practised in some parts of India, most contemporary chicas prefer to wear what they like. It's a great time to be a bride now, really. While global styles have permeated into the Indian psyche, there's also been a return to vintage in a big way, so you can wear anything from platinum and Venetian glass to your grandma's grand gem-encrusted jewellery.

Interestingly, the two most important trends in bridal jewellery are in opposition yet progressing simultaneously: minimalism and opulence. Some brides prefer to keep the jewellery light so it doesn't look unnecessarily ostentatious and can also be worn on occasions later, whereas others prefer to pile on all the traditional jewellery pieces and are even reviving some older ones, out of style for a few decades. These days, it's actually considered stylish to wear full-on traditional bridal jewellery, albeit not necessarily solid gold and hugely expensive. So, go for maang-tikkas in your parting, jooda pins in your French-rolled hair, kamarbandhs clinched around your waist, baajubandhs or armbands on your shapely, gym-toned biceps, several necklaces in varying thickness and length (choker, mid-length necklace, long necklace), earrings, nose rings, bracelets, bangles, anklets, rings, etc. And don't worry about looking done up. That's always in for brides.

Designs on design

If you're looking for some design inspiration, you may not have to go further than your movie hall. Bollywood, hitherto considered too showy and even tacky, is now quite the trendsetter. With so many fashion designers on the scene, it's not surprising that filmi fashion is now cutting edge enough to make the trendiest of gals want to take notes. Ishu Datwani, a partner at Mumbai's Anmol Jewellers, who have been catering to the trousseau needs of brides for the last 21 years, says 'Many come to us citing a particular necklace in the latest film. Sanjay Leela Bhansali's *Devdas* was a film that inspires women in their jewellery choices even today.'

Mridula from London, who had her big fat Indian wedding in Bhopal in April 2008, admits that she changed her wedding look at the last minute after seeing Aishwarya Rai's jewellery from Tanishq in *Jodhaa Akbar*. 'Luckily, I hadn't yet bought the big neck-pieces and earrings by then, so I was able to go for the Mughal and Rajput era styles in kundan. Paresh, my husband-to-be, laughed when he saw the haath-phool I'd bought too, but he was indulgent. I feel your wedding is one day when everyone forgives you going overboard!'

Heavy metal: Buying guide

Gold: Buy from a reputed jeweller and check certificates and/or trademarks. While 18k and white gold are stylish, the most popular type even today is a ripe yellow 22k. And do remember that the deep yellow of 24k is now considered old-fashioned and flashy by the fashion pandits as well as most jewellery lovers.

Other metals: Platinum is the most expensive metal chosen for wedding jewellery. Younger brides are wearing sterling silver and even stainless steel for less formal occasions.

Rolling stones

Diamonds: The wedding stone of the West, diamonds have become extremely popular among Indian brides today. Gorgeous, classy and contemporary, yet at the highest end

of the social status spectrum, they are indeed a bride's best friend (especially as one alterable set can be worn with several different outfits if need be!). Whether you're buying a simple wedding band with a few diamonds or a rock-encrusted dazzler, here's all you need to pick the right stones.

Learn to discern the difference between real and fake sparklers. Draw a straight line with a pencil. Put a cubic Zircon or an artificial diamond and a real diamond on it, and you will be able to see the line pass through the artificial diamond, whereas you won't be able to see it in the case of real diamond.

Check for the four Cs: cut (58 facets are good), colour (colourless is best though fancy 'coloured' ones are used a lot), clarity and carat weight (value usually decided by the size, but quality counts too).

Ensure that you don't buy blood diamonds or conflict diamonds, those made infamous in the 2006 film *Blood Diamond*. While there isn't an international assurance agency that can guarantee a conflict-free diamond just yet, enquiring about the stone's origins or asking for a certificate may give you an idea about its antecedents.

Precious and semi-precious stones: These days, rubies, opals, sapphires, emeralds, or even rose quartz, aquamarine, tourmalines and garnets are all becoming popular. The line between precious and semi-precious stones is now very thin, as a high quality semi-precious stone may cost more than a mediocre precious one. A good stone should have its original colour and clarity and be free of blemishes and cracks.

Big gems

The world's largest jewellery store lies on Chennai's Usman Road in Prashanth Gold Tower. The 70,000 sq ft retail space comprises two floors—one selling only gold jewellery, the other dealing in diamond and platinum—and over one million designs.

Great br-ideas: Purchase like a pro

Jeweller Ishu Datwani shares some insights:

* Wondering about quality and authenticity? A good jeweller should give you an authenticity certificate and show you the special hallmarking stamp on the item if you ask. Many, like we do, keep a karatometer on the premises. This shows you the purity of gold in 60 seconds and assures transparency in any transaction.

* A lot depends on your budget and how many sets you want to buy. A fairly basic one in diamonds for the reception, with matching earrings, bangles and rings, will cost you a minimum of Rs 10 lakh. If money's not a constraint, you can buy a mix of what's in vogue and the classic sort. (Wedding Belles note: Datwani means that if you have a small budget, you'd probably go for just one basic, less ornate set. Whereas, if you can spend more, you'll pick a mix of styles.)

What's trendy: This changes every one or two seasons. For example, in 2006–07, chunky sets in white metal like white gold with lots of multi-coloured stones mixed with diamonds were really popular. This season, we're seeing a lot of single-coloured stones (mostly either only-rubies or only-emeralds) mixed with diamonds. Also hot are only diamonds, or a mix of rose-cut and regular diamonds. And there's also a return to a golden finish and ethnic styles with stones, which will continue through 2008–09.

What's timeless: Some styles are eternal. Uncut diamonds are the epitome of elegance, whether you buy them in 1995, 2008 or 2025. The Jaipuri ones are really popular. Traditional designs, too, will always be a good choice for bridal jewellery.

Faux play

It may be hard to believe, but a lot of brides do wear fake gems, usually for the pre-wedding events, to add range to their jewellery collection, especially if they've gone all out for the main event. If you're going for this cheaper option, get the quality stuff (better craftsmanship, finish and polish of casing and colour and clarity of stones). Mix and match—wear a stunning necklace in real gold and gems, but armbands, rings, etc., in faux.

Bauble rap: Where and when to buy your jewellery

Engagement and wedding rings: These can be bought just a week or few days prior to the ceremony, as long as you have the right ring sizes. But when buying off the shelf, bear in mind that you may spend less time on the process but not always get the designs you're looking for. If you want to get them custom-created, order at least six to eight weeks ahead of when you need them to allow for unforeseen delays and last-minute alterations.

Mangalsutra: It may be tough choosing from among hundreds of designs, but this piece is most often picked from a store rather than specially designed. You can do this even a day prior to the ceremony, although we wouldn't recommend leaving it to the very last minute. Most times, the groom's family buys it, but it's best to discuss it in advance so that it doesn't get left out, both sides thinking the other's taking care of it.

Sets: A set usually consists of a necklace or choker, bangles in multiples of six, earrings and sometimes rings. If you're having a set custom-made, visit your jeweller as early into the wedding planning process as you can to ensure exquisite craftsmanship and finish. Remember, the shortest possible period for making a made-to-order set is about a fortnight. It usually takes longer than that, and the more elaborate your choice is, the longer it will take. Alternately, you could just pick a set from a jeweller's readymade section.

Go for gold

According to the World Gold Council, India is the largest consumer of gold in the world, with annual imports ranging from 700 to 800 tonnes!

Ask the experts

Jewellery designer and expert Poonam Soni, who has her own signature range and has been featured in the Italian fashion bible *Trends for Jewellery, Forecast 2009*, shares her thoughts on what gems are going to be hot.

What are the observable trends in bridal jewellery for 2008 and beyond?
For wedding functions, long earrings and thick, chunky cuffs are replacing more traditional looks. The less-is-more concept was not so popular for weddings anyway, but minimalism is officially out of the window. Ornate is in. You could go for just one piece, not necessarily expensive, but it has to really stand out in terms of uniqueness, size, design and colour. The lines between looks are blurring, for example, you could go for a classic-look set, but have it embellished in unusual materials.

Even for the big day, it's no longer about wearing 'safe' jewellery. Mixing and matching is good. Young brides are moving away from heavy pieces that scream money and towards biggish, ornate statement pieces that are rich in Indian craftsmanship.

Can you predict which metals and precious stones are going to be hot?
Typical gold is out. The style statement today is to wear a combination of three–four different types of gold. Uncut diamonds and jadauu work is a perennial favourite that won't stale in a hurry. Wearing large, single colour sets of rose-cut diamonds is a big trend. Rubies, emeralds, South Sea pearls, jadauu tukdis... these are all going to be the mainstay of upcoming weddings.

The look calendar

Six months prior

Eat healthy.

Work out at the gym or indulge in at least 30–45 minutes of aerobic activity three times a week.

Use sun block and tan protection.

Follow the three steps of skin care diligently: cleanse, exfoliate, moisturise.

Six weeks prior

Scale up your fitness routine.

Try skin brightening or polishing treatments if your dermatologist recommends them.

Drink lots of water.

Make sure you're getting enough sleep, not stressing too much.

If you're going to have a major haircut, do it now—if you don't like it, you've some time to let it grow out and/or adapt it to your look.

Six days prior

Get all the parlour essentials out of the way: facial, waxing, threading, bridal massage. Manicures and pedicures too – or move just these closer to the date of your first function if you think your nails might chip.

Book spa treatment; this is when you should be putting your feet up. Take some of your bridal team along if this will make it even more fun!

Six hours prior

Before any of the occasions, ensure you've got enough sleep.

Place used teabags or cucumber slices on closed eyes for about 10 minutes to soothe any tired lines or puffiness.

Use a mild scrub or ubtan (home-made or store-bought) so that your face doesn't show any traces of make-up or dead skin cells.

Rinse with cool rose water.

Hair and make-up: get help from a trusted parlour, or do it yourself.

Pale? Here's a tip from model-turned-actor Milind Soman: 'I rarely use any products, but if you're looking pale or tired, you could use a touch of bronzer to add a healthy colour to your face like I do.'

Six minutes prior

Check for spinach or other food between your teeth.

Have a small sip of water — and a breath mint.

Refresh your lipstick or gloss.

Use a compact or loose powder in case you're perspiring.

Check for strays in your hairdo

Check that no labels have been left on, no straps are showing.

Moisturise your hands.

Dab perfume on your wrists, behind the ears, in your cleavage

Get your bashful bride smile on and you're ready to go!

Great br-ideas: Wedding day emergency kit

'Be prepared' was your motto when you were a girl guide at school. So when it's an occasion as important as your wedding day, you know you're not going to take any chances.

* Extra shoes. Keep a pair of comfy neutrals on standby just in case the special ones you picked start to give you shoe bites or come undone.

* Band-aid and gel pads. To ease shoe bite and burning soles on days when you have to stand to greet all your guests.

* Extra make-up. Just the basic touch-up kit so that your lips don't lose their gloss and your post-bidai, tear-stained cheeks can be repaired.

* Sewing kit. With threads that match your outfit just in case something snags or comes apart at the seams at the last minute. And little scissors to snip off hanging threads.

* Duct tape and cello tape. The heavy duty, double-sided sort, just in case some aspect of the décor needs to be affixed. The more delicate, transparent type for emergencies like holding a reluctant flower the right way up.

* Safety pins and hairpins. Your grandma or favourite aunt may have them hanging on her necklace, as always, but better to make sure you've got a few extra on hand. You never know when an outfit or hairstyle is going to give way!

* A tiny mirror. To discreetly check for imperfections that need to be attended to.

* Personal products. Deodorant, perfume, hair spray, toothbrush and toothpaste, breath mints... anything you think you'll need to stay fresh.

* Lots of tissue paper. For wiping away smudged make-up, food particles, other people's lipstick marks from your cheeks, etc.

* Stationery. Pen, paper, Post-Its and tape (in case you need to post a note somewhere).

* Phone numbers of everyone: wedding planner, decorator, caterer, etc. So you can nip a glitch in the bud before it becomes a crisis.

Brush with beauty: Hair and make-up

Today's bride does just as she pleases, playing coy or cool depending on her mood. Her wedding outfit allows her the freedom to move around and she's usually the life and soul of the party, playing confident and gregarious hostess at her own reception. She may dress modestly or go the ultra-glam, backless-choli way, and she'll definitely have her head uncovered and her hair done up beautifully. Also, these days, now that bridalwear isn't about covering up and hiding your face, more than ever before brides have to pay particular attention to how their hair's done, as well as have impeccably applied make-up.

Different strokes

Wondering how to coordinate your hair and make-up with your wedding outfits? Concerned whether what suits you and what's in style might not necessarily be the same thing? We give you a few quick-fix options based on the latest trends and your bride type (remember that Bride Quiz you took on pp 65-6 to determine this?).

Traditional: Opt for a simple bun, perhaps embellished with flowers or jewellery. Make-up in mostly pinks and peaches, with deeper tones for shadow and blush. Lips can match your outfit, but watch out for harsh reds and magentas that may make your lip line appear severe. Best for the pheras and other formal, traditional rites.

Great br-ideas: No tress distress

Murphy's Law: If everything that can go wrong does, there's still hope. If you're having a bad hair day and the stylist's best efforts aren't helping to tease your tresses into some semblance of order, go for the two easiest options. If your hair's short, use gel to wear it sleek and off your face. If it's long, tie into an elegant chignon at your nape. Dangle a maang-tikka or add embellishments like sparkly clips or a fresh flower (provided your ceremony's not longer than four hours) and voila! Also, soothe angry acne with a cover stick. Your stylist will take care of the rest.

Girlie: Frame your face in soft curls held back with a jewelled barrette or two. Or go Greek Goddess with hair cascading down your shoulders and a slim golden band or braid at your temples. Make-up is fresh and minimal, with natural tones, lots of gloss and shimmer. This works especially for less formal functions like cocktails or the youngsters' party.
Glam: What goes best with your dipping décolletage and uncut diamond set? A Swarovski crystal-studded head and lush make-up, of course. Also try twisty blonde extensions to add oomph to your jooda or crystal ones to up the glam quotient of your hair. Dramatic gold-maroon, green-purple or rust-peach shadow and plumped up, moisture-drenched lips add to the allure for that sangeet or reception.
Experimental: Hair off your face is the first tenet of bridal style in India. So, obviously, you're going to want to break that rule at least once during your wedding week. An asymmetrical fringe, lots of body and a bit of unruliness are the perfect ingredients to stir up some fun at the youngsters' party or hen night. Make-up can feature unusual juxtapositions of colour, near-Goth style or anything new that's caught your fancy.

Choosing a stylist

Go by word of mouth rather than picking the one with the best PR. Get friends and extended family to share their experiences. Pick the stylist that suits your budget as well as your schedule. Meet with him or her to check your comfort level. Does s/he get your vision for the wedding day look? Do you speak the same language when it comes to style? Do you need to go to the salon or will s/he make home/hotel visits? Does s/he come across as a level-headed person who will stay calm even if traffic held you up so long that the baraat's at your doorstep and you're just getting started? Will s/he be on call throughout your functions or will you have to wait endlessly while a celebrity client is being attended to? Find out if trial runs are included in your wedding package, or if you'll need to pay extra for them. If you're working with a group that has many stylists, ensure that they're going to send you the same stylist on the day of your wedding that you meet with in advance, and not send an assistant.

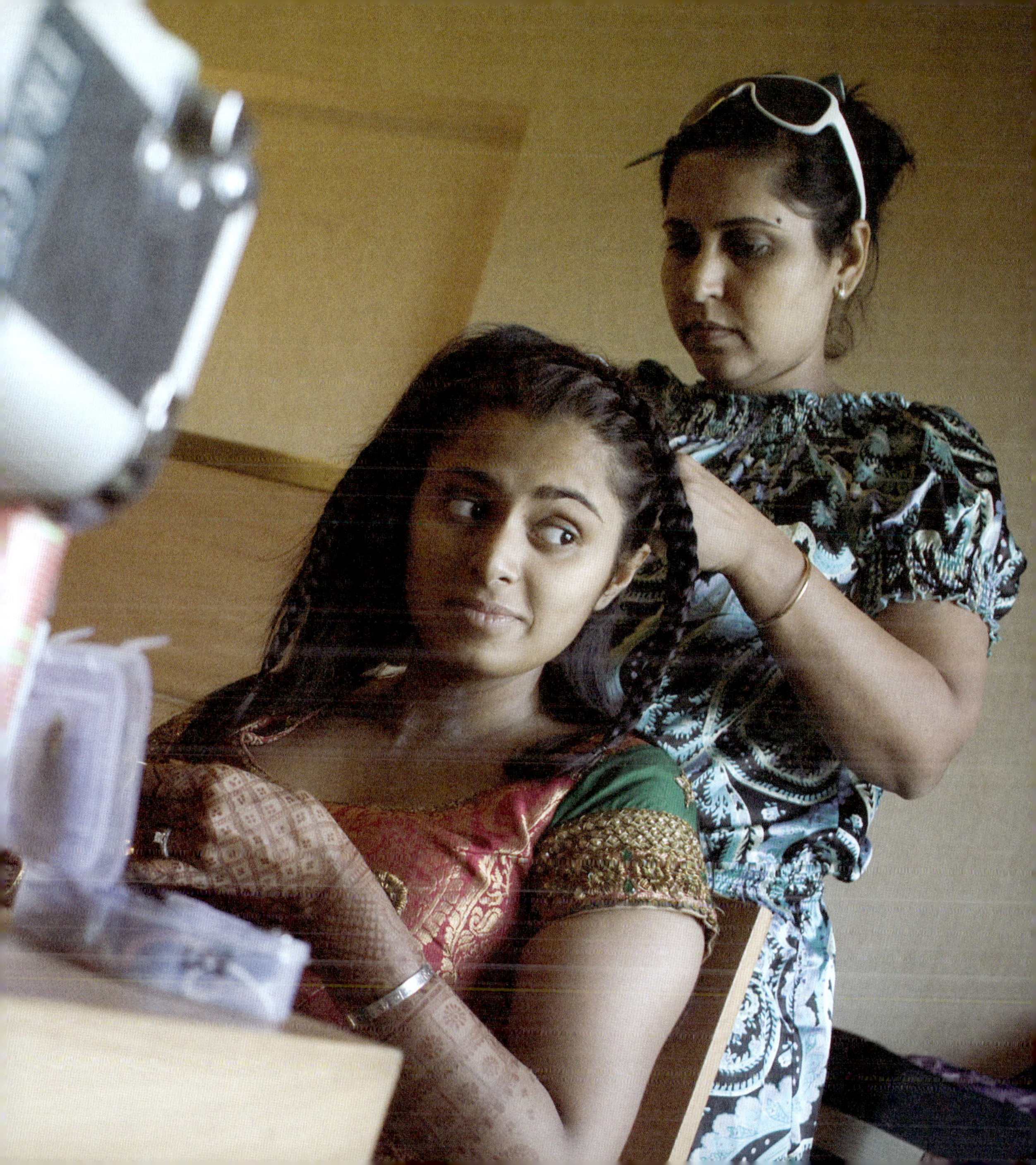

Make it clear right from the start that there's room only for one diva at your wedding—namely, you. Convey to the stylist that creative tantrums and tardiness will not be tolerated, however good he or she is with the blow-dryer or the blush brush.

Tip: Make-up man Tilak R. from Ahmedabad recommends that you budget at least four hours if you're going for a moderately elaborate hairstyle and basic make-up. As you know your wedding date and the various occasions well in advance, book the stylist as soon as possible. Also, identify a back-up, in case your designated stylist is unable to make it.

Planning

Speak to your stylist in detail about exactly what you have in mind for each day's look. Take magazine images or printouts from websites to illustrate. If you don't have a clear picture of what you want, ask your stylist to suggest some styles, and perhaps do a trial run (or two) to make sure you like the way the proposed style turns out.

For make-up, do a patch test early on to ensure that the brand s/he uses is compatible with your skin. Explain whether you want light, medium or really heavy make-up. These days, a more natural look, with glossy lips, is preferable to the matte, mask-like look finished with truckloads of powder that was previously in vogue. When you do the trial, ensure that the look is suitable both for photos (you want to go a trifle dramatic here), as well as for interacting closely with your guests (more natural).

How important is it to follow fashion diktats? Not too much, really. And bridal make-up and hair are usually toned down and prettified versions of what's in vogue anyway. Freelance hair and make-up expert Recinda Martis from Mumbai, who works on six to ten brides a week during the peak wedding season, says, 'Global and national trends are important, but only as very basic guidelines. What I concentrate more on is giving the bride a fresh, clean look that projects her own personality and highlights her best features. At the end of the day, she has to be comfortable to carry off the look I give her.'

Sharing is caring

- If you share your stylists with other members of your wedding party, do so smartly.
- Decide on a person who has a number of competent assistants (send a friend on a mission to the salon or on location to see how they work) and make sure they bring them.
- Budget time accordingly, giving yourself first preference—you needn't feel guilty!
- If you have the time and energy, work out a flow chart that factors everyone's needs in.
- If you want your best friend by your side—synchronise appointments.
- Ascertain early on whether you're personally going to pay for all the services.

Fit to wed

Every bride wants to look beautiful, with that newly acquired love glow. The key to looking your personal best is a proper fitness and eating regimen, and adequate sleep. Do a few stretches daily to keep limber and eat a nutritious, non-toxic diet.

Even if super-svelte is not you, getting toned will help you look your best. Most gyms advocate a maximum weight loss of three kilos a month. Three to six months before your nuptials is the best time to start getting into shape and if you have one to two months in hand, you can tone your abs, biceps and back (most likely to be seen once you don your wedding finery). Gyms now offer special prenuptial packages for brides. Like Moksh in Mumbai where a Bridestar package costs Rs 50,000 a month and includes gym membership, personal training, yoga sessions, and a diet plan. Some gyms may even relax their timings or fit you in at odd hours. All the world loves a bride-to-be, after all.

Skinny to shapely

If you're super slim, you might actually want to gain weight before your wedding. But don't start bingeing on bananas to fill out your fabulous designer lehenga. Eating an unusually fattening diet may lead to oily skin or worse—acne—so desist from downing dried-fruit milkshakes, even if family and friends try to thrust them upon you. What you can do is hit the gym. No, that's no joke... a lot of gyms have weight gain programmes, although they aren't publicised as much as the shed-kilos-today variety. Work out under a personal trainer, follow a diet plan and soon, even if you may not be as pleasantly plump as you wish, you'll have some muscle definition and maybe even bulk, roses blossoming in your cheeks and the glow that every bride craves.

Working out a workout schedule

This might be even tougher than the workout itself. If you're involved in all the nitty-gritties of planning the wedding yourself, you may not have time to take those six km power walks you planned, unless your dress designer's going to run with you, trailing swatches. If it's high-impact stuff you need, sign up for a thrice-weekly boot-camp. Many gyms offer sessions that last about an hour and challenge all the muscle groups with a varied and high-energy workout. We advise you advocate extreme care—it wouldn't do to be hobbling around your havan with a muscle pull or having to sit out the dances at your party because your knees are screaming blue murder.

If you prefer something less aerobic, try pilates, a programme of low-impact exercises and stretches, often done on specialised equipment. Offered at some gyms or through personal trainers, pilates gives you a thorough workout without your even realising it and leaves you rejuvenated rather than done in.

The middle path would be to enrol yourself and hubby-to-be for salsa classes a few months ahead of the wedding: a good way to get fitter, have some fun, and relax in each other's arms. Although Sandip Soparrkar, India's most well-known and internationally qualified ballroom dance expert, warns, 'Yes, joining a dance class with your significant other is wonderful but some couples who are first-time dancers land up squabbling a lot!' But fiery fights burn calories too, don't they? And you could wow your guests when your DJ plays a few salsa numbers at your sangeet.

Food for thought

Even as you may want to restrict your calorie intake in a bid to lose some last-minute inches, we suggest you keep in mind that the wedding week is a stressful and extremely active period. You will be constantly doing something. The exertion, as well as the emotional enormity of the life-changing step you're taking, is likely to take a toll. Avoid fainting spells and other embarrassments by eating sensibly. If nothing else, grab a muesli bar or a bowl of yogurt and chopped fruits. This is not the time to starve and try to lose that last quarter inch—you'll probably lose a few kilos without changing your eating habits at all. Your body needs fuel (maybe even more than usual) to keep you going.

Ask the expert

Fitness guru Ramma Bans advises: 'Do not fall for fad diets such as only-liquid or only-pineapple diets, crash diets, pills and powders. A girl who came to me once had followed some papaya diet which had resulted in her face breaking out into eruptions. This happens a lot because people can be quite stupid and blindly follow some fad.' According to the fit-at-80 Ramma, who has coached the likes of actress Rekha and several Miss Indias, the best way to lose weight is over a longer period. 'Walk, do floor aerobics, yoga and lots of stretching, in tandem with a healthy, nutritious diet that is devised according to your body chemistry. I believe in the ayurvedic system, which believes that the constitution of each body is different, so what works for one person may not be effective for another. Go to an expert, and answer the 28 questions to find out whether your body type is vaata, pitta or kapha and get a customised plan which you can stick to.'

Bedtime tales

All wound up and having trouble sleeping? Here are some sleep enhancers to help you into the Land of Doze...

* Meditation. If you're not a regular meditator, keeping your eyes shut and attempting to clear your mind of clutter is sure to get you drowsy after a while.
* Soothing music.
* Counting to the high numbers.
* A relaxing aromatherapy massage with lavender oil.
* Putting a cushion under your feet or between your knees (or whatever position works for you).

Sleeping duty

A large part of looking your best is getting the right amount of sleep. Not too little and not too much (as if there's a chance of that, if you're part of the organising committee!). Eight hours of shut-eye may be an optimistic hope, especially if your boss hasn't granted you any leave and you're still micro-managing the minutiae of your wedding plans. Six to eight hours is optimal every night, and is especially crucial during the last week before your wedding.

Don't sacrifice this, even if it means delegating or dispensing with some extra details that might have added to the wedding, like tying those bows on the chairs just the way you want them. You don't want to look raccoon-eyed on D-Day, and what will hundreds of people be photographing and commenting on—you or the chairs? Keeping the big picture in mind is of the essence.

Go with the glow: Skincare

Is the glow love or Dove, everyone asks. Bridal skin is perhaps the most discussed cliché. How do you ensure your radiance is perceivable during the various wedding functions?

Here's a plan to perfection: Inside outside

For starters, inner happiness is important. Your skin will show signs of stress and lack of sleep, so pack up all your worries and spend 30 minutes a day doing something you really enjoy. Listen to upbeat music, dance, read the funnies, meditate, watch a sitcom (and stay OFF those cranky serials and sad movies), bond with your pet... basically, do something that isn't at all wedding related.

Peel spiel

Most Indian cultures incorporate haldi or turmeric paste into the ritual cleansing before the wedding, as we consider this natural antiseptic auspicious. While haldi kaa ubtan is de rigueur, other aspects of the skincare routine vary. A good homemade face pack is a two-third–one-third mixture of multaani mitti (Fuller's Earth) and rose water for oily skin and the same mitti with milk for dry skin. Apply the paste and allow it to dry and harden. Then scrub the mask off to exfoliate the dead cell layer. Other popular options are besan (chickpea flour) and malai (cream) or sandalwood powder and rose water.

Also, all the commercial face packs, masks, peels and scrubs that you can buy over the counter at any multi-product store, chemist or spa shop: apricot, walnut and strawberry scrubs, Dead Sea mud packs, orange peels, things that can seemingly defend you from everything—age lines to alien abduction! Be adventurous but we wouldn't recommend trying something new very close to your wedding in case you have an adverse reaction.

Bride bright

Although we think that dark is just as beautiful, we realise there's often a lot of pressure from parents and peers for brides to appear as fair as possible. But isn't it better not to obsess about skin colour, and celebrate the one you have? Making the most of your complexion could entail a basic cleansing, exfoliating and moisturising routine, a home bleach if you're used to doing that or else a professional facial. There are also a number of services that help to eliminate tanning and rejuvenate skin that's been exposed to the harsh elements.

And it's not just about the face. Dr Snehal Sriram, Head, Medical Services, Kaya Skin, observes, 'Sunlight on the back of the hand causes tanning since most people neglect to use sunscreen on their hands. And the palm is subject to constant friction and exposed to allergens. Despite the fact that the skin on the hands is thicker than that on the face and can take a lot of wear and tear, it does get damaged too. Our Hand Shine service (which uses micro dermabrasion and a glycolic peel) is becoming quite popular with brides-to-be. But we do it only in select cases, when the client needs it and we are sure she will ensure proper post-care in terms of protection from sunlight, etc.'

Ask the experts: A guide to being a brilliant bride

Dr Snehal Sriram, Head, Medical Services, Kaya Skin, shares her recos for the latest bridal beauty treatments.

* Treatments like skin polishing, brightening or even lightening help reverse the damage the sun wreaks on your skin, especially your tan. But it's most important to adhere to an appropriate skincare routine for the long-term. Using sunscreen, cleansing, toning and moisturising, will ensure your wedding day glow doesn't fade in a hurry.

* Protect your skin with a sunscreen (minimum SPF 15) during the day.

* Nourish your skin with a good recharging cream (preferably containing jojoba oil or vitamin E) at night.

* Hydrate your body internally by drinking lots of water and having foods that are rich in vitamins A, C and E (papaya, carrot, lime juice, green vegetables).

Relax to the max: Spa services

Bridal nerves need super soothers It's a fact that the wellness industry has noted and acted upon. No wonder there are so many spa services specially created to relax and rejuvenate you, the glowing bride. So how do you know which one will work best for you? Shop around.

Access: Look for something close to home. If it feels like halfway around the world to get there, remember that it'll be just as far going back. Instead, spend a little more if you have to, but go to that fabulous place closer home.

Attitude: Snootsville is not a great place for spa therapies. If the reception staff acts high-handed, walk straight out. Massages and spa treatments require a certain heightened level of service that not just touches your body but also your soul. If they're busy giving you superior glances, they probably aren't going to be very professional in the therapy room either. Friendly, warm, anxious to please, is the sort of vibe you need to feel.

Hygiene: Spas as they are usually high end, adhere to world norms. But do watch out for the tell-tale signs that all is not well.

* Greying or stained towels and linen indicates falling standards.
* Wet or dusty work areas could be rife with germs.
* Places that aren't well ventilated could leave you with a headache at the least and breathing problems at the worst.
* If products used are not hypoallergenic, your sensitive skin could react badly.
* Therapists who lack personal hygiene can be really dangerous, apart from making for an unpleasant experience.
* Diseases can be harboured by massage tables where towelling is reused.

Don't just sign up for a rose facial because that's all that's on offer, if you absolutely abhor roses. Find something that appeals to your mind as much as it attracts your watch, your wallet and your physical well-being. If you love aqua pura, try an Evian shower. If wine's your poison, how about a grapeseed extract exfoliation? If you can't live without chocolate, perhaps a chocolate massage would do the trick? Pamper yourself to the max.

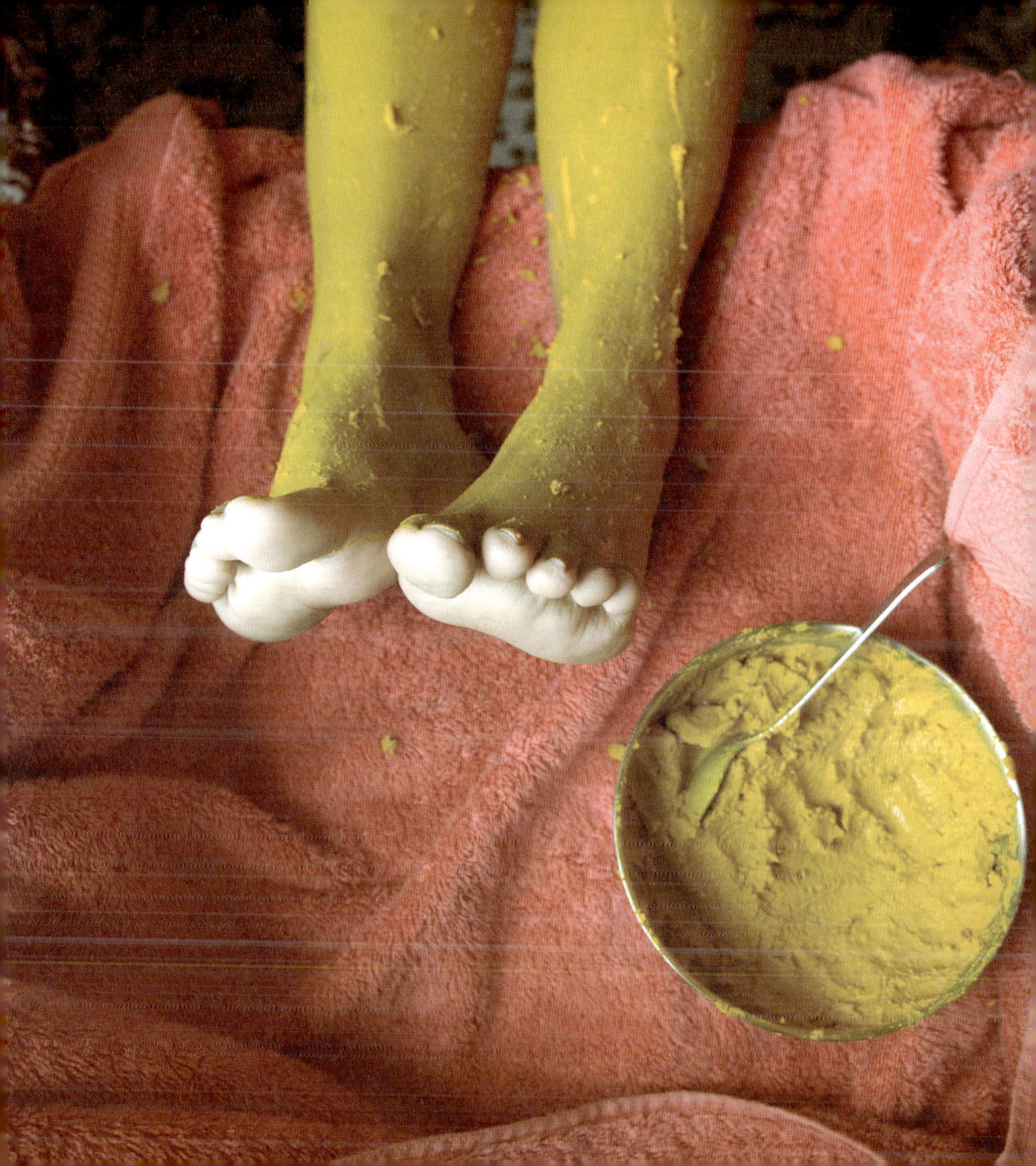

Shiny, happy people: Diamond facial at Blush

The Blush range of clinics in Mumbai has a full-fledged bridal package, but Dr Pai's Diamond Facial, which uses diamond dust as an exfoliant, is increasingly high on brides' must-do lists. Now you can literally be 'badan pe sitaare lapete hue' like the song.

The treatment begins with a back massage with moisturising cream. Then a minty cleanser, followed by soothing zinc-based cream, which readies your face for the special diamond scrub to come. The scrub is a gentle yet gritty goo, comprising tiny motes of diamond dust that work to remove dead skin cells very effectively. Steam and specialised massage strokes help boost the scrub's effects. Soothing cream is reapplied after the diamonds have done their work, after which a green apple mask is applied to cleanse the skin. This is followed up by a serum capsule concentrate and then an algae peel-off mask.

Dessert for your face: A super-luxe diamond cream massaged deep into the skin with the use of a galvanic ioniser. And the afterglow? It's called the Diamond effect.

For Blush contact information, see our vendor listings on p 275

Where's the Party Tonight

Pre-Wedding Events

Chances are that your wedding festivities won't be a one-day affair. But hey, you'd love to celebrate your wedding every single day for a month (or even longer), and enjoy all those colourful rituals. Whether you're thinking intimate or magnificent, there will be pre-wedding parties or ceremonies that you'll plan just as carefully as your big day. These additional functions and rituals play a special role in your wedding—they extend the good times, allow you brief but guilt-free stress-busting opportunities, and give family and friends from both sides a chance to get to know each other.

We love a good party—so in this section, we'll guide you through the logistics and planning that go into throwing fabulous shindigs before your actual wedding.

Most Indian weddings are at least two–three days long, with a line-up of events that joyfully embrace revelry and tradition. (There are exceptions to this—some weddings last just one day, like Malayali weddings, whether Christian or Hindu.) In a multi-day wedding, some events have a religious flavour like the Mangalorean Christian ros or the haldi ceremony (a must for most Hindu and Muslim brides). Some are age-old customs that symbolise the bond of marriage in a fun and evocative way, like the mehendi. And some—like the let-your-hair-down hen party, or everyone's favourite event, the sangeet—are just for the mazaa of it!

Although the mehendi and sangeet parties were originally north Indian wedding traditions, many brides from other parts of the country are now choosing to include these functions in their festivities. Who can resist a night of foot-tapping music and uninhibited dancing? Or a cosy afternoon with relatives and friends, nibbling on scrumptious snacks, and having beautiful henna designs patterned on to your palms or arms? These events make a bride really feel like a bride, and give everyone else yet another occasion to rejoice in a couple's happiness—and show off another beautiful ensemble.

Planning and budgeting

You and your family will decide which types of pre-wedding parties you're going to host as you're creating your larger wedding budget (see chapter Where's the Party Tonight: Pre-wedding Events, pp 31-45). You'll have to weigh the number of guests and the scale of the whole wedding, what your religion and customs require, what your parents want, and what you want. For example, is an engagement party a must-have event for you, or is it better to slip your pennies into your piggybank for the actual wedding? Should you splurge on a pre-wedding sangeet or cocktail party, and skip the big reception after the wedding ceremony? Wouldn't it be prudent to combine the sangeet with the mehendi because they both need a DJ and a dance floor?

Note: since friends or sisters usually host some pre-wedding events, like the hen party or bridal shower, you won't need to account for those parties in your budget.

The guest list

Pre-wedding functions are a great area for compromise in terms of the guest lists. If your parents are taking over the main day, maybe you and the groom can influence the sangeet and perhaps the mehendi as well. So whip out your Auroville handmade paper notebook, that filofax or your Excel spreadsheets and get started! You and your family should start making your pre-wedding parties guest lists at about the same time you're working on the main wedding list. Make your biggest party list first, which includes everyone. Then you can pick out the ones you want to repeat and the ones to call for just the one big event.

So which guests usually come to which parties?

For hen nights and bridal showers: a bevy of chosen women from the wedding party.
The mehendi: traditionally a ladies' function, but in recent years both men and women close to the bride attend.
The sangeet: usually a selection of closer and more important wedding guests.

Sangeet as the main event

Turning convention on its head, having a large sangeet and a smaller wedding is becoming a popular trend among brides today. Some couples find that intimate wedding rites feel more special because their guests are actually listening to the ceremony; so much nicer than having a large group gab noisily and knock back the drinks, looking for a waiter to grab some chilli cheese toast from!

Kaveri and Anshul from Bangalore invited the majority of their guests for their cocktail party at Herbs and Spice, a medium-priced, open-air venue outside the city, and kept the actual wedding ceremony very small and intimate—partly because Kaveri was paying for the sangeet, and also because they wanted to cover everyone on both their lists. Importantly, their wedding venue, the Leela Palace poolside in Bangalore, allowed a limited number of people on the main day, so it made sense to have everyone at the sangeet.

Different events, different sizes

We suggest varying the size and scale of your parties, even if you're lucky enough to have a bottomless budget. Having some exclusive events with interesting themes will make your wedding more distinct and memorable—and more fun for your guests.
Here are some ideas for working your guest list:

Invite only older family members and your parents' friends for an intimate religious ceremony or traditional pre-wedding function. They'll probably appreciate the event more than your younger guests. And not only do they often help understand the significance of a ritual, but older people at, say, the manja ceremony at a Muslim wedding, or the janavasam at a Tamilian wedding, can give good advice on how the ceremony should proceed.

Invite only the younger lot to a less formal get-together where they can dance the night away. This is perfect for your mehendi or sangeet, or an unconventional costume or theme party that you and your fiancé really want to experiment with. Many guests remember these party events as the best part of a wedding.

Invite one of your groups of friends to come together for a separate event, even if you're not calling them for the main wedding functions. Call your guests from abroad for a luncheon at home. Meet your yoga group for a last pre-wedding yoga session and afternoon tea. This way, you have more time to personally interact with your special guests—and they're still a part of the festivities.

For a five-day extravaganza, most brides create one big wedding invite that contains separate cards for each function, sending some guests all of the cards, and others just the cards for the events they're invited to. (See our information on wedding stationery on p 54).

The pre-wedding look

The bride's aunt rushes to find the bride, who's sitting with her hair in curlers as her best friend's sister is doing her make-up for the sangeet. Her harried aunt announces that the dupatta the bride is to wear, with a fishtail lehenga and brocade corset, has just been scorched while being ironed. Crisis! The bride has to wear the dupatta or the outfit won't be complete—what's more, her in-laws will be aghast at her brazenness if she goes without it. She feels her heart sink. Just then, her sister jumps up and rushes off. She is back in five minutes—holding an old georgette sari of their mother's from the 1970s, in the exact same shades as her lehenga. Together, the girls wrap the sari as a long dupatta around the bride, pin it in place so she can dance a little (not too much wild boogying—she'll save that for her own sangeet). Voila— the bride's a stunner!

You're the ultimate style diva, why should your wedding be any different? You've spent ages dreaming up your wedding day, knock-out outfit. But don't forget that you actually become a bride a few days before the actual wedding day; you need to be your perfectly turned-out self at your pre-wedding parties, too. Here are some tips for making sure you shine at the sangeet and dazzle at the dance party, preparing the world for your grand entrance on the actual wedding day and feeling at ease while you're at it. (For more on how to lead the 'most stylish bride' list, check out chapter Getting the Wedding Belle Look, pp 63-76.)

Dress for the occasion. Don't lose sight of the basics: temperature, time of day, and activity tempo. Do you need a halter blouse for a June bash, or heavy silks for January? Is the event a brunch brouhaha or a late-night soirée? And will you be in boogie mode or standing demurely for numerous hours?

Dress to fit in with your guests. Work out how heavy/light, conventional/daring, traditional/modern your look should be for each function by taking a peek at the guest list. You don't want to scandalise his grand-aunties with backless cholis, or feel like you're burdened with a heavy lehenga if all your friends are hanging out in casual kurtis or jeans.

Dress yourself in different designers, or switch your styles. If you're a designer diva, you know that a Rohit Bal cocktail ensemble gives you a completely different look from a Sabyasachi wedding lehenga, which will in turn be very unlike a Manish Arora skirt and corset outfit for your mehendi. Even if you're not into labels, think different styling, embroidery, and cuts for each outfit—you don't want to be a Sridevi, who seemed to think varying the colours of her chiffon saris did the trick!

Dress using accessories and styling tricks to create different looks. Sonia Vohra, a wedding stylist from Bangalore who's dressed over a thousand brides, always finds different ways to drape the bride's saris, arrange flowers in her hair, and change her make-up colours for each day so she never has to repeat a shade of anything. Vohra also uses the bride's different sets of wedding jewellery to create the tone for each overall look. Kundan works beautifully with pastel colours, and antique gold brings out the zari in traditional saris. Heavy choker necklaces look fabulous when your hair is up for that princess look, and long, south Indian gold necklaces look elegant with a low chignon.

Dress to match the colours and themes of the events. If the sangeet décor is white chiffon draperies and jasmine flowers, be a delicate queen in white. If the reception is Rajasthani-themed mirror work, reds could make you a beautiful and ethnic just-married.

Dress with your timeline in mind. If you only have two hours to get dressed between your wedding ceremony and your reception, keep your different looks simple and not too hard to change between. Trying to convert a bouffant into a sleek open hairdo might be difficult (and stressful) in 20 minutes, even with the best hairstylist in town at your disposal.

Real-life Wedding Belles Share Their Pre-wedding Look

Kavya, an ex-model from Bangalore who is now a designer and media professional, had an interfaith marriage with multiple functions, so she varied her hairstyles to help create a different look for each event. 'My hair is naturally curly. I left it open and natural for the mehendi, tied a high ponytail and let the curls run down for the sangeet, tied it all up in a bun for the Arya Samaj, and straightened it out and left it loose for the wedding blessing and reception,' she recounted.

Let's Get Together: The Engagement Party

All eyes are on the lovely girl in a shimmering blue ghagra and her handsome almost-fiancé, dressed in a sharply-cut soft grey suit with the red tikka on his forehead. The groom reaches into his pocket, and the bride gasps. The ring is an antique diamond set in dull gold—his grandmother's ring. She looks at him, realising perhaps for the first time that she now belongs to his family, too. The ring matches her wedding jewellery perfectly. And because he's made the right choice, she knows she has, too...

The first prenuptial celebration you'll probably plan is an engagement party. Yes, you'll want a chance to flash that ring—not to mention that new fiancé. Sizes and styles of engagement parties vary hugely—from family-only aashirvaad affairs that bless the betrothed couple to the more public (call the neighbours in!) engagement party.

Types of engagements

In more conventional north Indian Hindu families, especially if you're having an arranged marriage, the two families may want to seal the deal quickly with a puja and a party. Hindus call this roka, which literally means to stop looking further. Although it's not a mandatory Indian tradition, the couple sometimes exchanges rings on this day. The families usually exchange gifts like jewellery, saris, and sweets. The actual north Indian formal engagement usually takes place a few days before the wedding, heralding the start of the wedding festivities. Called the mangni among Muslims, sagaai in Uttar Pradesh and Rajasthan, the misri among Sindhis, and many other names in different communities, this ceremony has the couple exchanging rings, followed by a party.

South Indian Brahmin communities, like those in Tamil Nadu, have a formal engagement ceremony soon after the couple decides to get married—often months before the wedding. A priest draws up a formal marriage agreement, which he places on a plate along with bananas, coconuts, and betel leaves. Both families accept and agree on the date, time and venue of the marriage, then exchange traditional gifts like sweets and fruit. The groom's family usually gives the bride a sari.

Bengalis have a special engagement ceremony called ashirbaad, which happens about two days before the wedding. The purohit conducts a ceremony at the bride's or groom's home, centred around an idol he brings with him. The bride's family pays a visit to the groom and blesses him in the presence of the purohit; the groom's family blesses the bride. The families light lamps to give the proceedings a festive air, and elders bless the couple. During this ceremony, the groom's family gives the bride a sari, a ring, and other gifts; the bride's family gives the groom a ring, gold buttons, and a watch.

Other groups like Muslims and Roman Catholics have a ring ceremony at home or at a party, which features a blessing along with the exchange. The engagement party can be large or intimate, as dictated by budget and community protocols.

Pointers to help you and your families celebrate your engagement

When

Most engagement parties happen just before the wedding in India, though nowadays some happen right after the proposal, or in the period between the proposal and the wedding. Some people also combine the engagement with other wedding festivities—such as the sangeet or the mehendi—to reduce the number of events.

Who hosts

The girl's parents usually host the engagement party—though financially independent couples may pay for the party themselves (and thereafter, the wedding as well).

Who attends

Do you want your coming together to be blessed by everyone at a big bash? Or would you rather gather your families for champagne and dinner at the best restaurant in town? No rules here, as long as you work with what both families want and budget for.

How

As you're creating your vision for the party, be sure to talk to your parents, his parents and other family elders about religious and community traditions for the ceremony, food and décor, as well as their personal preferences. Their inputs, your ideas, your budget, and guest list will impact whether you decide to have immediate family at a small ceremony followed by a meal at home, or a bigger affair and a party so large that you'll need to hire a venue, a caterer, and possibly a decorator to do flowers, lights or even a theme. (See our chapter Behind the Scenes on how to work with these vendors on pp 195-232).

Don't get overwhelmed by all the advice you're going to get at this time—everyone's as excited as you, and sometimes even more so. It's good practise for the actual wedding!

The look

You'll probably wear traditional clothes if you're having a ceremony of some kind. Do dress up—but a word of caution: make sure you don't go so overboard in your enthusiasm to look bridal in your engagement outfit that it becomes a case of the bride overshadowing the bride. You want your bridal outfit to be the one that shines brightest.

The rings

If you're a classic dresser, a slim ring with a solitaire setting, or one main stone surrounded by baguettes, is both elegant and forever stylish. For your groom, the classic understatement of the gold band is the ideal choice. Go with a platinum band for a really sophisticated look.

Sharad Kumar of Pratibha Jewellers in Bangalore counsels that engagement rings be durable. Have your ring made by a diamond setter, with solid setting and at least six prongs holding the stone in place. If you're a weekend rock climber or are frequently in situations where you might bump your ring against hard surfaces, pick stones with less vulnerable points and a hardy setting, like a bezel setting (here the stone is flush with the ring's surface). (Or plan to keep it off your finger, in a safe place. Might sound like we're being paranoid, but believe me you'll want your ring, like your marriage, to last a lifetime.)

If you enjoy a bit of glamour, go for new cuts, like that of the Zales Diamond (from the famous store of the same name), with eight sides and 82 facets which accentuate the sparkle. Another popular new shape is the princess cut (also called the modified square), designed to get maximum brilliance from a square cut so it stands apart from traditional round, marquise, emerald, pear, or oval shapes. The tension setting, where the stone is on by its edges and so appears to float, makes a sleek, modern statement.

Right now, 'the real trend is to be different', says Kumar. He's been getting many requests this last season for hammer-finished mixes of gold and platinum, and combinations of

gold and rhodium. Antique rings are also popular, in tune with the vintage trend of the moment, but so are minimalist, clean lines in modern designs. And coloured diamonds and oval shapes are all the rage with brides, too, Kumar says.

Deepti Sudhindra, an independent jewellery designer who runs The Jewelry Project in Bangalore, says that brides today have a huge choice. 'Many brides are now interested in rings that are funky and different. I customise rings according to the personality of the couple. People come to me to engrave their names, the date they met, or even poetry on to gold and silver rings to use as their engagement bands. It's about making a fashion statement, yet not spending too much on it.' In her last collection, she put kundan onto gemstones for a completely new look. She suggests combining your community's traditions (for example, the ruby and old-gold mandatory in the south, or the ubiquitous jadau in a north Indian bride's trousseau) with modern designs to create a unique piece.

Another trendy design option: his and hers rings that come as a set or complement each other—though this assumes that your groom will be happy about wearing his ring after you are married! But don't sweat if your guy is fussy about wearing jewellery; you can convert his ring into a piece of jewellery for yourself later by melting it down or making it into a pendant, or simply resizing it to fit your finger, if the design is neutral enough!

You might get two rings for yourself from the start if you decide to follow the Western custom (an engagement ring and then wedding bands). Consider an engagement ring and wedding band that go well together. A solitaire diamond ring works beautifully with an eternity band of diamonds—both can be worn on the same finger. Or, two rings can be clipped on together to make one bigger ring.

Most jewellers will create and deliver your ring in 1 to 3 weeks, depending on the design.

Girls Just Wanna Have Fun: Hen Parties, Bridal Showers and Mehendis

Because you could never have gotten this far without the women in your life. Hen parties and bridal showers have a special way of making the bride feel loved and beautiful, and are all (or mostly) girl oriented—because good, old-fashioned girlfriend fun never goes out of style.

The bride's sisters or closest friends usually do the organising for the hen and bridal shower parties, and mothers and aunts pitch in for the mehendi. You might have one combination party thrown by your gal pals, or all three if budgets allow. The planners of these parties can go crazy on funky themed invites and risqué party favours (see pp 135-41)

And they can decide to invite just the girls—or let the boys in if they beg. Enjoy these get-togethers—they will probably be the most relaxed time you have until you disappear into the sunset!

Best of cluck: The hen party

Your last round of single fun with your gang of girls. The hen party is becoming a very popular part of the great Indian wedding. Essentially the girlie equivalent of a bachelor party (your fiancé's pals will probably plan something rowdy and raucous for him), a hen party can be theme based or consist simply of a wild night of bar-hopping. Many shy away from it as they think it can only mean a night of total debauchery. But we also have alternatives for a hen day, night or weekend, with activities you and your friends will enjoy.

When

At least two weeks before the wedding. Having it during the wedding week might spell trouble—you don't want to be hung over for the mehendi lunch.

Who hosts

The bride's sisters and closest friends. Guests pay their own way and chip in to treat the bride, though best friends and sisters can choose to shoulder more of the costs. If the group plans to split the bill, say the tab at a spa or bar, the hosts should ensure that everyone can spend the same amount; a very chi chi place might be difficult for the bride's younger working girlfriends, for example. Keep a buffer for last-minute drop-outs or unanticipated costs (like that extra tray of test tube shots), or better still, collect a kitty up front or afterwards. A hen house party can also be potluck.

Great br-ideas: A surprise hen party

A surprise party is always a good idea because it's so fun. But the hosts should keep a party outfit ready for the bride to change into, so she isn't caught in her grungy tracks for her special night out on the town.

Who attends

The bride's closest gal pals, sisters and female cousins. We suggest inviting only girlfriends and family you feel most comfortable with. You'll be engaging in some harmless, licentious behaviour, flirting with cute bartenders, and generally being a drama queen, so you don't want an envious colleague or a censorious sister-in-law-to-be to cramp your style. If your fiancé or future MIL is pressuring you to invite his giggly cousins, be firm. Give them special mehendi day duties or have a family lunch to placate them, instead.

The look

Costumes for the bride or the whole gaggle are a sure-fire way to get things started—giggles guaranteed. Try harem pants and veils, Playboy bunny ears, naughty badges or matching T-shirts. And what's hen night without memorable giveaways? Interesting hen night favours are available at the local smuggler's market (see p 140). Think wicked!

How

The hosts should plan the event based on what will help the bride de-stress and have the most fun. Is she shy or a wildcat? Does she like sophisticated wines or is she a tequila shot maniac? Would strippers shock the life out of her, or will she get up and boogie with them? Would she prefer a lounge day at the spa, or a naughty night out? Would dinner at a swanky hotspot like Olive be her idea of fun, or a weekend roaming the malls of Bangkok be the ideal hen trip?

Great br-ideas: Have a hen weekend getaway

Hen getaways work best a few weeks or months in advance of the wedding, as the bride will need plenty of time for last-minute wedding details before the big day or week. Hosts should also fix the date for the bash far ahead to give guests enough notice to coordinate their schedules and plan travel. Try sending out a trial group mail with a few dates to see which would get the best attendance.

What kind of hen are you?

Take this quiz to find out what your ideal hen party should be like:

Your idea of a fab Saturday night is:
a) A bottle of wine and candlelit dinner
b) Bar hopping till you can't see
c) Camping out in the jungle and watching the sun rise

In 'Sex and the City', the character you identify most with is:
a) Carrie
b) Samantha
c) Err...*Sex and the City*? What's that?

What do you do when you get together with your girlfriends:
a) Shopping and manicure
b) Partying and checking out the action at all the city hotspots
c) Pyjama party with ice cream and old romantic movies or five seasons of '24'

Your idea of adventure is:
a) Teaming the new Chanel tunic with those cool tights you found on Janpath
b) Dancing a salsa number with the cute waiter at a formal dinner
c) Exploring an East European city without a map

Your home is:
a) A large closet for all your clothes and shoes
b) A place to pass out and nurse evil hangovers
c) Your castle, your pride and joy

You get most shocked by:
a) Bad taste
b) Nothing
c) Exhibitionism and excess

Mostly a: You're the Princess Hen. You believe in enjoying the best in life. Your ideal hen party would be a posh dinner, or drinks at the city's most elegant nightspot, or indulging yourself on a shopping spree.

Mostly b: You're the Rocking Hen. You are the life of every party and will probably fill that role at your own hen bash. You're that girl dancing on the table and singing at the top of your lungs. Your ideal hen party would involve large amounts of alcohol, strippers and maybe some kinky toys.

Mostly c: You're the Chilled Hen. You are a relaxed and personable bride with lots of friends who love hanging out and doing regular things. Your ideal hen party would be one of the alternative ones—adventure sports, a weekend getaway in a beautiful woodsy retreat, or a barbecue on a friend's terrace complete with a guitar and much singing.

Theme ideas

Some fun ideas below! Let your theme influence decorations, food, games, costumes, parting favours and more. (Tip: These work well for a bridal shower, too.)

- Arabian Nights: Harem pants, veils and dupattas draped across your living room; hookahs and falafel, and a stripping sultan.
- Bollywood item number girls: Give Rakhee and Katrina a run for their money in skimpy bling outfits and wriggle your stuff to the song of the moment.
- Village belles out on the town: Bring out those cotton skirts and silver jewellery, match them with sari blouses and dupattas. Balance some matkas sexily on your hips.
- 1970s or 1980s fashionistas: Get the disco beat going with gold jumpsuits, afro wigs and *Saturday Night Fever* at a nightclub or at home. Mirror balls mandatory!
- Flower children: Commune with flower power in mom's bell bottoms and your big shades. Download some cool retro tracks from Woodstock and feel the good vibrations.
- Teen pop stars: Try a Britney in tiny skirts, big hair and goth eyes.
- Cowgirls: Dolly Parton could be your inspiration to look hot even in a checked shirt, jeans, boots, and a Stetson. Pile on the country music and hire some horses!
- Baywatch: Red swimsuits and blow-dried hair, and lots of pouting on the deck of a private pool. You'll be Pam Anderson in Pune!
- Miss Universe and her retinue: Bring on the ball gowns. Buy tiaras from a local toy shop or a costume jewellery store, make sashes with strips of satin, and walk through the bar or the party blowing kisses, thanking God and promising world peace.
- Angels and devils: Wings and haloes, little horns and tails from chart papers

- *Grease*: Dress up as different characters from the movie. You could be Sandy, Frenchy, or Rizzo. Send everyone home with copies of the film with your face and your fiance's face photoshopped over Olivia's and John's on the CD cover.
- Schoolgirls on the loose: get naughty with school uniforms and pigtails.

Unusual hen party ideas

If the bride isn't the bar-hopping type, here are some hen ideas with a difference:

* A day at the spa (see our listing section on p 262 for some great pampering spots in your city)

* Adventure sports like bungee jumping and rock climbing for more daring brides

* A yoga weekend in a quiet, natural place to get you ready for the crazy days ahead

* A day of shopping at your favourite mall (this could be combined with the shower—everyone could buy the bride's gifts at the hen party, or give her gift certificates to use there)

* A picnic in the countryside, or an excursion to the nearest sanctuary or wildlife park. A resort weekend in Coorg, Panchgani, Neemrana or Ranthambore

* A spa weekend at The Vedic Village Spa outside Kolkata, or Shreyas near Bangalore

* A 2-day houseboat cruise on the backwaters of Kerala

* A camel safari in the Thar desert

* A dance class where you all learn how to salsa from a professional dancer

* A glass-shattering karaoke night at home or at a happening nightspot (cocktails, to loosen up your vocal chords, are optional)

Games

Whether you're partying at home or at a bar, these games are sure to entertain, whether you want to get naughty or be nice.

Naughty: Confessions

Get each hen to write a question that she's always wanted to ask the bride. Then make the bride answer the questions, the more embarrassing the better. Place a tray of shots in front of her—if she answers a question truthfully, she's let off—but if someone calls her bluff, she has to have a shot. And if she can guess who asked her the question, it's that hen's turn to have a shot.

Nice: Good advice

Cut chart paper into heart shapes and attach a straw to the back of each heart with tape so it looks like the straw is a stem hanging down from the heart. Ask each guest to write her 'advice for the bride' on a heart. (For example: Never go to bed mad. Have your husband's favourite dish for dinner once every few weeks—just because ... Go to bed in a slinky negligee at least once a week.) Place the completed hearts on straws in a bowl or vase (they'll look like an arrangement of flowers) and ask the bride to read them out loud. Not only is this heart-melting stuff of which bonds are made, but you also create a great keepsake for the bride.

Naughty: The bride's last blast dares

If the bride refuses to do these, she has to be punished! Shots of particularly strong spirits like tequila and vodka are the standard scare. To add to the merriment, if the bride rises to the occasion and completes the dare successfully, her friends should have to do a shot, or do the next dare on her behalf. The best places to do the dares are in a bar or restaurant so you can involve innocent (and not-so-innocent) bystanders of both sexes—if you're brave enough. Otherwise, even a private venue is good enough to embarrass the bride and provide cheap thrills to her friends and sisters!

Some sample dares:

- Act out your favourite Kama Sutra pose for 15 seconds
- Exchange your clothes with one of the other hens in under one minute (you can decide how far to go!)
- Sing '*Like a Virgin*' Madonna style, standing on top of the bar
- Pretend that a cushion is your favourite film star, and kiss it in ten different ways
- Confess the wildest thing you've ever done
- Eat a banana in a suggestive way—or to get even saucier, put a condom on the banana with your mouth
- Get a leash, put it on the hottest guy in the bar and walk him like a dog around the room
- Talk about your sexiest asset for one minute
- Describe (or act out!) your most secret fantasy
- Dance like you're on MTV grind for one minute
- Pretend to be Karishma, choose your Govinda (a man if you're in a public place, otherwise choose one of the girls) and do a pelvic thrust Bollywood number for one minute.

Nice: Guess the giver
Have everyone wrap their gifts in special paper that means something to them, without a label saying who the gift is from. For example, if I collect teddy bears, I would wrap my package in teddy bear paper and Mom could wrap hers in paper with pictures of the bride through the years on the package. The bride then has to guess who each present is from.

Naughty: Pin the willy on the body
This can be great fun if you tie it to your theme—David Hasselhoff's face on a sketched-out body would certainly enhance your Baywatch hen party.

Nice: The soon-to-be-wed game

Ahead of time, ask the groom a list of questions about his relationship with the bride (the more personal the better—it doesn't have to be entirely 'nice'). Some examples: When did you first meet your fiancée? What did you do on your first date together? What are your favourite parts of your fiancée's body? Then have the bride guess what the groom's answers were and see how many of her answers match his (plus how embarrassed she gets!)

Favours

Favours aren't compulsory, but it's always a nice touch to send guests home with a small gift. And in the case of hen parties, it's easy to play on your party theme, or give gifts you know would tickle the bride. (See our Vendors guide, pp 262 for ideas on where to source these.)

- Small wine or champagne bottles: label with the name of the bride and groom, and the date they will be married. Both classy and unique, a real winner.
- Small seedling tree or flower seeds: great for the green-conscious bride. Each guest can plant a tree in honour of the bride and groom. Or give each guest two or three packets of seeds, placed in a decorative pot.
- Mirror-work or ethnic boxes, or batuas filled with things naughty or nice.
- Pot-pourri: make little pouches of it in the bride's wedding lehenga colours.
- Plastic handcuffs: fun for all and available at some toy shops or your local smuggler's market. If you want the real thing in metal, in Bangalore you can try the Gujjri Market opposite Russel Market, or in Bombay perhaps check with a friend who works in film.
- Bracelets: get name beads for each guest and string them together for a cute giveaway.
- Bath accessories: elegant gift packs of aromatherapy massage oils, lotion, scented soap.
- Candles and essential oils: again gift wrap these or present them in a basket.
- Chocolate or candy willies: a speciality chocolate maker can attach a name card to each.

Real-Life Wedding Belles Remember Their Hen Parties

'It was the sweetest, most fun party ever! My girlfriends got together, baked an obscene cake, compiled a host of naughty games and bought me lots of lingerie. What made it all so special is the effort and love my friends put into making it a night I'll always remember.' —Arati, Bangalore

'I had two hen parties—one was a surprise thrown by my own friends which was an all-red party red decorations, red drinks, red clothes. I was blindfolded and led there. The second was thrown by our common friends; my groom was dressed in drag and brought in to surprise me!' — Kaveri, Bangalore

'The hen party was a surprise and organised by my very good friends at a friend's house. The theme was Harem Nights. All my good friends were there, and that's what was special. The décor was organised by the hostess, and drinks and food costs shared between all the girls.' — Nisha, Bangalore

'My friends arranged it as a wonderful surprise. I have a mild obsession with, or rather an addiction to, chocolate and I didn't have the time for a weekend getaway. So my two best friends arranged a chocolate and champagne workshop with this eccentric Italian lady in Notting Hill, London, where I was living then. The event was made special by the fact that it was a complete surprise but lovingly done, my passions kept in mind. Gorgeous sexy nightdresses as presents and just the right number—ten of my close friends, meant the world to me!' — Suruchi, Bangalore

Swinging in the rain: The bridal shower

The bridal shower is an old custom in the West, where the bride is literally 'showered' with gifts to jumpstart her married life. It can be an alternative or an addition to a hen party.

When

Any time before the wedding.

Who hosts

A friend or family member of the bride.

Who attends

The bride's women friends and family. Showers can accommodate multiple generations (the giggling cousins you didn't want to invite to your hen party!). A larger party could include sisters, friends and other female relatives from both sides, plus lots of fun gifts. A smaller bash could mean quality time with only your closest girls, with time to ooh and aah over wedding gifts—and party on afterwards.

How

Hosts can spice up the proceedings with games. (See games listed earlier in this chapter under hen parties.) Everyone congregates around the bride as she opens up her loot.

Great br-ideas for the bride at her bridal shower

* If you're opening gifts in front of the group, get some quick acting tips to pretend you simply love that Pyrex bowl or gilt candle stands that just aren't you.
* When you're on present number 25 and some of your onlookers start to lose interest, don't feel pressured to rush through the rest. Enjoy opening them.
* Don't forget to say thanks. Show your hosts how much you appreciate their efforts by bringing them a little gift to the party. Little photo frames with pictures of all of you, or tiny earrings are good options, also thank you notes or a call the next day.

Great br-ideas for super shower gifts

Gifts for the home, music you know the bride will like, voucher for a spa day, or lingerie are always welcome presents at a bridal shower, but try our ideas that are sure to surprise.

* Scrapbooks and recipe cards: Bring a lump to the bride's throat with a book of favourite photos and memories. Send everyone a page to decorate and then bind them together in a book to present at the shower. Or collect favourite recipes in a fancy box so the bride can have all of her friends and family help in her new married kitchen.

* Have all of the guests bring gifts based on a theme: If she's a star chef, have everyone bring a gift for the kitchen, or if she has a good sense of humour then a gift for the bedroom. Do an ABC's shower, where each guest gets a letter or two to represent with their gifts. Or an around-the-house shower, where each guest gets a room to bring a gift for.

* Make a honeymoon care package: If the bride is getting ready for a week on the beaches in Bali, stuff a waterproof bag with sunglasses, sunscreen, fluffy towels, flip-flops, a hot bikini, books and magazines.

* His and Hers: Embroider the bride's and groom's first names on matching bathrobes (it will be like they never left that fancy honeymoon hotel!), or their new monogram on bath towels.

* Soon-to-be: Get a T-shirt or hooded sweatshirt for the bride that says/incorporates her new last name. Like 'Mrs Khan', or 'Soon to be Mrs Bachchan.' It's sure to get a great laugh with gaggle of girls –and she'll be just like Britney Spears, who sported a 'Mrs Federline' tee when she got married.

Henna, bolo bolo: The mehendi party

It's almost impossible for someone to believe you're an Indian bride if you don't have those intricate mehendi designs on your hands and arms. The mehendi tradition is 5,000 years old—and its importance for north Indian Hindu and Muslim brides across the country is undiminished. Some say this beautiful practise originated in Africa, others say it was brought to India by the Mughals. In all of these cultures, applying the crushed paste of the henna plant symbolises fruitfulness and good things to come, especially when it adorns the hands and feet of a new bride (and in some cases, a bridegroom, as well).

Such is the allure of mehendi, that when we spoke to brides from Bangalore and Assam, Bengal and Kerala, we found that many of them had added mehendi to wedding celebrations even though it hasn't been a part of their tradition. We can't blame them; besides being auspicious, we all have to agree—mehendi looks just fabulous. And it's a lovely way to feel pretty while bonding with the girls.

When

Families usually plan mehendi parties during the week leading up to the wedding day. Mehendi is best applied in the daytime; sunlight makes the fresh, bright colours of the flowers, clothes and bangles come alive—a photographer's feast. A daytime party also works best for a mehendi because it gives the bride more time for application and drying—which can sometimes take a few hours.

A Muslim bride, however, will often have a mehendi ki raat, which is combined with the sangeet and includes traditional music and dancing by hired performers or the family.

Great br-ideas

Try some vodka golgappas—they go down nicely on a long, lazy afternoon.

Who hosts
Usually the bride's mother or aunt.

Who attends
Mehendi parties were traditionally small and intimate, with just the female coterie of the bride and the groom. Nowadays, however, most people mix it up—close family and friends are both invited, and this includes both men and women.

Where
Use a little imagination and you can create a mehendi venue anywhere—at home, in a beach shack or in a hotel. You just need divans or mattresses, maybe a big wooden swing for you to sit on while your hands and feet are being adorned, and space for lots of dancing. And of course, a good team of skilled mehendi artists. (See Behind the Scenes on pp 227 for tips on how to source mehendi artists.)

How
At a mehendi party, the bride usually sits in an area decorated with fresh marigold and jasmine, attended by at least two artists decorating her hands and feet with exquisite patterns. At the same time, the assistants of the main artist work on the palms of girlfriends, sisters and other female family members. The crowd dances to traditional mehendi songs or favourite Bollywood mehendi songs (see next page), while snacking on chaat, drinking lassi or cocktails, and choosing colourful bangles and bindis to match their outfits.

For Muslim brides, the mehendi is the biggest, most important pre-wedding event. The family of the bride blesses the henna with a prayer, and sometimes the future in-laws buy the henna and send it over for the event. The mehendi function happens separately in both the groom's and the bride's homes. It is frequently combined with a party that is equivalent to the sangeet, with live musicians performing ghazals and other songs. In some Muslim families, the girl's family visits the boy's side after the dinner.

Food

Tangy chaat and scrumptious snacks are perfect, light treats for this time of pre-wedding bridal adornment. But remember your guests and you will need to have your hands free while applying the mehendi and while it dries—so make sure guests have the opportunity to eat a bit before getting started, or that someone comes around to help feed them a bite every so often. This is when a little nephew or niece can come in handy!

Ask the experts: Sample daytime mehendi menu

(Courtesy Soneelam Chodha, Queens Restaurant, Bangalore)

Papdi chaat
Bhel puri
Pav bhaji
Dosas
Rasmalai or kulfi
Masala chai
Paani puri
Aloo tikki
Chana bhatura
Vegetable or chicken rolls
Malpua and kheer
Jaljeera/ Lassi

Music

It's customary to play Hindi movie songs or traditional wedding songs. You can get a CD made in advance, download and plug in your iPod, or get a DJ who knows his mehendi music. Traditional Punjabi, Gujarati or Rajasthani wedding music is easily available.

The Top 5 mehendi songs (as compiled by DJ Jasmeet, Bangalore)

'Mehendi laga ke rakhna', *Dilwale Dulhaniya Le Jayenge (DDLJ)*
'Mehendi hai rachnewali', *Zubeida*
'Mehendi hai rachnewali', *Kal Ho Na Ho*
'Bhumbro', *Mission Kashmir*
'Bole chooriyan', *Kabhi Khushi Kabhi Gham (K3G)*

Favours

Bangles and bindis for all the guests are a must. You can add a feeling of ethnic authenticity if you bring in a lac bangle maker or an actual churiwala, like Suruchi did when she got married in Rajasthan in 2006. Another creative bride, Neha, a marketing professional, made little silk pouches for the favours in bright colours like red, green and blue, with gold work. Neha also gave her guests little decorated mirrors—a last, perfect touch.

Some of our other favourite favour ideas: little boxes, scarves or dupattas, silver or bead jewellery, and wedding song CDs. You could make the favours more casual—one bride had fun shirts made up of the bride and groom with their heads Photoshopped over Bollywood/Tollywood actors and actresses. The guests wore them during the mehendi.

Great br-ideas to splurge or save on

Splurge: Give Swarovski-studded bangles as takeaways.

Save: Decorate your own silk scarf favours with sequins or fabric paint. Pair them with glass bangles, and present them together artistically.

The look

You can decide if you want to be the traditional bride-to-be in a ghagra or heavy salwar-kameez—or if you'd rather kick back and feel comfortable in three-quarter-length jeans, with an embroidered chunni thrown over your shoulders to stay faithful to the ethnic feel of the mehendi. Typical mehendi colours are bright oranges or reds, but greens and rust are also on the palette and good for hiding any stains. Consider yourself warned.

Gouri Kapur, a Bangalore make-up artist and stylist, recommends ghagra-cholis highly. They are best for the trendy mehendi look, accentuated with simple daytime make-up. Even if you're going for the full-on bridal look, keep it light so you can have fun and dance. Wear half-sleeved or sleeveless tops. Tie your hair up so it's out of the way.

Real-life Wedding Belles Dress Up

'I wanted a lime/mint green outfit for the mehendi, so my best friend Namrata and I designed the mehendi outfit together—a brocade printed green corset and a lime green, full-length panelled skirt with brocade piping. The skirt was lined with bakram net to give it bounce.' — Kavya

Party mix: The sangeet or the cocktail party

The word 'sangeet' means music in Hindi, and that's just what makes this, for many, the queen of all pre-wedding events. (Thank you, Bollywood!) Historically, the sangeet was an occasion for the ladies of Sindhi and Punjabi families to get together and sing lots of naughty and politically incorrect songs to the beat of the dholak or other traditional instruments. The extempore rhyming and hip-shaking dancing could have taught Saroj Khan a thing or two (no men there, so the women really let go).

The get-together lasted for several days before the wedding and was a chance for the ladies to dwell on the lighter side of marriage, making light of all the intrigues and family politics the new bride and groom would have to deal with in their life together. In the Gujarati community, the sangeet traditionally involves the dancing of the beautiful garba and dandiya raas. Rajasthanis sing folk music related to weddings. South and east Indian communities haven't traditionally had this function at all.

Now sangeets have evolved into larger dance parties, where the men also get in on the fun. Hired musicians, like qawwals or ghazal artists, usually perform, followed by a DJ playing the latest Hindi movie remixes to keep the dance floor pumping until the wee hours. Many communities that don't have sangeets, traditionally, have happily adapted this idea of merrymaking, and many families across India now hold a pre-wedding cocktail party that they call a sangeet or a cocktail party. Christian brides sometimes have a cocktail party before the wedding as well, though the music usually consists of a live band crooning classic English hits or a DJ playing international numbers—with a few exceptions where Bollywood has prevailed. The Muslim mehendi function combines the elements of the sangeet and the mehendi.

The sangeet is one part of the wedding that the couple's personalities sets the tone for. It can be a laid-back and relaxed lunch barbecue with the groom acting as DJ, or a 500-strong bash at a palace, planned to the minutest detail.

When

Most sangeets are in the evening, but afternoon or luncheon affairs work as well. Most families fix the sangeet about two days before the main wedding— by when all the important guests who are coming for the wedding will have arrived (the guest lists for these two events usually have a large overlap).

Tip: If you're planning to party hard at your sangeet, choose a date that's not the eve of the wedding. Dark circles, a champagne headache and swollen feet from six hours of dancing won't help you look your best for a 5 a.m. puja.

Who hosts

Traditionally, each side had their own sangeet function, with their own families attending. But more and more, couples are combining sangeets/cocktails to save costs, and because guest lists overlap.

Who attends

Who you invite to your sangeet depends on how you've planned your wedding events. Traditionally, the sangeet included the most important wedding guests, but you may decide to make the sangeet bigger than your more intimate wedding day function. (Some couples make this a 'youngsters' party because of the copious drinking and debauchery which are the mark of a truly successful sangeet.)

Where

You can vary the venues for your sangeet/cocktails from hotels and farmhouses to homes, beaches or even palaces in Rajasthan. All you really need is a dance floor, a good music system, an open bar and a strong desire to have a blast. Importantly, the convenience (and bargaining possibilities) of having the sangeet in the same venue as the wedding is something that you should consider.

Entertainment
At an old-fashioned sangeet, the bride's aunts and sisters would dance informally, and sing typical wedding songs that have been in the family for generations. But today, you can make your sangeet much more exciting and entertaining for your guests. Hire a choreographer and get all your friends to do a rehearsed dance—you could all be Ash in a flash. (Check out our guide to working with choreographers on pp 220-23.)

Direct a skit making fun of all your relatives or describing your beautiful love story in uncensored detail. Hire a celeb DJ or book the city's best singers. Put together a slide show or a film of the best and worst moments in your lives growing up and as a couple. And if you're keen on performing yourself (or your in-laws are into Bollywood and expect you to do a Preity-style '*Maahi ve*' number), make sure you dress light and practise hard.

After the classical musician (or Kareena Kapoor—because if you have the budget, you can get a Bollywood star to perform at the sangeet) finishes performing, make sure you get a good DJ who knows about wedding-compatible music and can handle a gazillion requests. Give the DJ a list of your favourite tracks or artists in advance so you don't end up with electro-trance when you want the latest Shah Rukh tune. (See our guide to working with DJs on pp 224-26).

Or you can go the other way—especially if you have a smaller sangeet—and be your own DJ, ensuring that the retro mood or *Umrao Jaan* theme you've created for the sangeet carries through in the music, too. Sasha, an entrepreneur from Mumbai, says, 'We pretty much doubled up as DJs. We were just very particular about what we wanted so we decided to do it ourselves.'

Food and drink
The food for the cocktail party or sangeet should be different from what you serve on the main wedding day. Importantly, if you're a Hindu or are from a community such as that

of Kerala Christians, you may not be able to serve alcohol or even meat on the main day, so you can go to town on these for the pre-wedding party, most likely to the satisfaction of your guests. Also, heavy starters are a sangeet staple—they work well with the cocktails you'll be serving.

If you hire a bartender service, have them whip up fresh, fun, juice-based cocktails for your guests. You could even make a signature drink or two for the bartenders to pass around with a clever name, like Marriage Martini or something that plays off the couple's new shared last name (a Khan Cooler or a Gupta Gulp). Your guests will love your creativity, and you may even be able to save on alcohol costs if your bartenders mix the signature drink ahead of time with cheaper brands than you'd want placed out at the bar.

Give your bartenders instructions about when and how to discreetly close the bar. And point out any relatives or friends they should be on the lookout for—especially prudent if you have an Uncle Rajeev who's famous for undressing in public after his fifth drink.

Décor

Match the décor to the colour of your outfit, or go with the trendy décor of the moment. Everything ultimately rides on your taste and spending power. If you're into the simple and elegant, fresh flowers and bandhini dupattas will do the trick. If chandeliers and elephants are your style, go with a decorator who can fulfil your most decadent, outrageous desires. (See our guide to working with decorators on pp 203-05)

The look

A sangeet is less formal than the wedding, and so most brides use it as a chance to be more experimental, daring, or contemporary with their ensemble than they'll be on the actual wedding. Lehengas are the right way to go, for easy movement and the variations they offer. Some brides even wear heavily embellished Western-style gowns.

Real-life Wedding Belles Remember Their Sangeets

'I wore turquoise blue and dull gold for the sangeet. The outfit was designed by Seema and Jamila Malhotra. They made me a beautiful fishtail skirt in dull-gold brocade, silk fabric with turquoise blue borders on the waist and at the bottom. The top was short with a scoop back and completely embellished with antique gold threads, blue crystals and antique gold sequins. I have worn the outfit many times since my sangeet! Samir wore a Nehru collar black jacket with formal black trousers'—Kavya, Bangalore

'I had bought an outfit from designers Anjali and Arjun which was blue with silver, so I matched the decorations with that using blue orchids and silver net. The event was special since we had close people, and had an evening of dances performed by my friends and family for Gaurav and me. I had organised the dance bit and chosen songs which told everyone a story about how we met and fell in love. We had practises for about three weeks before the final performance.' — Neha, Delhi

'Raghava [the groom] designed the entire look and feel of the cocktail party which was at the Taj Residency in Bangalore. They gave us the entire floor, so we had two rooms and a hallway. The hallway was a street scene with pushcarts, fortune teller, tarot card reader, cotton candy, etc. One room was a stage with a huge painted backdrop of me and Raghava. The other room was only for the buffet.' — Netra, Bangalore

Cocktail couture cues

- Take in these tips from Bangalore stylists Sonia Vohra and Gouri Kapur:
- Make sure your dupattas are pinned in place.
- Ensure that your hair is up, so it stays put even if you decide to headbang to Himesh's latest.
- Use matte make-up to avoid the unsightly sheen of sweat, unless you want to consign your wedding pics to a box under your bed. Blotting papers (The Body Shop sells them) are also useful, or just regular tissues, discreetly tucked into a handy, embroidered or brocade purse.
- Don't overdo the contouring and concealer for your make-up because you're going to interact with people up close—emphasise eyes and lips more, as they're what will stand out both in conversation and in pictures.
- Experiment with a slightly more Indo-Western or contemporary look for this party if you're planning to go traditional on the wedding day.
- Stick to darker hues and a sleeker silhouette as much as possible—this will make you look every inch the glam heroine for the night.

Great br-ideas to splurge or save on

Splurge: Suruchi, a lawyer who comes from an NRI London family had an engagement and sangeet two-in one event, set against the stunning backdrop of Jaigarh Fort, Rajasthan. Live music from Anaida, Sukhbir and DJ Aqueel rocked the party until morning. Guests enjoyed free-flowing alcohol, caviar flown in from her father's Moscow office, and great entertainment in the form of a skit.

Save: Kaveri, a hands-on bride who designs clothes and light fittings in her spare time, created a magical feel by doing the flowers and lights herself.

Religious/Ritualistic Pre-wedding Events

Even if we tried, it would be impossible for us to cover more than a small percentage of the functions in Indian weddings, as they could take up the space of a few books all on their own. So consult the older people in your family, the family priest, or your wedding planner to get your rites right.

But here are a few of the important religious pre-wedding events that are special for different Indian communities.

Wedding traditions

In a Muslim wedding, the bride's father accompanies the maulvi to seek her confirmation for the nikah from their religious head and a senior family member.

The haldi ceremony

Common to many religions and regions is the haldi or ubtan ceremony (as it is called in north India) to cleanse the bride and groom before the wedding. The same ceremony is called manja among Muslims, and ros among the Catholic coastal communities like Goans and Mangaloreans.

The haldi ceremony usually happens on the eve of the wedding or two evenings before it, either separately in the homes of the bride and the groom, or at joint parties organised by the two sides. It consists of a religious blessing, after which family members and community elders anoint the bride or groom with a paste made of turmeric, rose water and sandalwood, or sesame oil, depending on the custom of the house. This ancient practise originates from the days when aunts and sisters applied this paste to the skin of the bride and groom for weeks before the wedding, to cleanse and cool their skin and add a glow to their complexion. The deeper significance of this ritual is that their souls were being cleansed, as well. Today, in addition to blessings, well-wishers give the couple gifts.

Different communities and religious groups have different variations on this ceremony. Gujarati couples wear old clothes which are then symbolically torn off to signify a new start in life. Then, traditionally, the couple don't leave the house until the wedding day. Catholics usually have a fun party after the ros. In fact, for Bombay Christians, this ceremony, called the paani, is an accepted alternative to the bachelor or bachelorette party.

Planting a tree (mandav saro)

A Parsi bride and groom perform this old Zoroastrian custom four days before their wedding. Each of the two families plants a young sapling (usually of a mango tree) in a pot of soil enriched with betel, turmeric and rice. The priest recites prayers, and the pot is placed at the entrance of their homes. The family waters the plant every morning till the eighth day after the wedding and then transplants it elsewhere in the home, praying for a peaceful marriage for the couple.

Ceremonies on the eve of the wedding

To begin the wedding on an auspicious note, most communities have a blessing or puja officiated by a priest the day before the wedding, either at home or at a place of worship. Syrian Christian Malayalis have a special ceremony called minnu kettu in the boy's home the day before the wedding. The boy's maternal uncle teaches him the art of tying the minnu (or thaali, mangalsutra) by twisting three threads of a cotton sari belonging to the bride-to-be together with a little starch. The groom will have to demonstrate this skill the next day in church when he ties the minnu on his bride.

Syrian Christians, as well as Hindu Malayalis, also traditionally hold a gurudakshina ceremony the same day at the groom's and bride's homes, during which the parents on both sides give the elders in the family a betel leaf and a token sum of Rs 101 each.

Gujaratis hold the sagri ceremony on the day before the wedding at the bride's house. The female relatives of the groom visit the bride, bringing flowers, cosmetics, and jewellery. These gifts for the bride are a sign of affection and acceptance, and symbolise the new relationship between the bride and her future in-laws.

Juroon is an Assamese function that requires the groom's mother to go to the bride's house with her female relatives and give the bride presents like fish, sweets, and clothes and jewellery to dress her up. The groom has no part in this particular ceremony, which is usually followed by a big lunch party.

A similar function is common at Sikh and Hindu Punjabi weddings, called the 'chunni charaan'. The bride is given 'suhag ki pitari' (a decorated basket containing gifts from the groom's mother). These gifts usually consist of mehendi, clothes, jewellery, fresh fruit and dried fruit, dried coconut, dried dates, bangles, sindoor (vermilion powder that married women use in their hair parting to indicate that they are married) and a red dupatta. During this ceremony the ladies sing wedding songs to the beat of a dholak.

Bengalis celebrate the eve of the wedding with ai budo bhaat—the bride's last meal in her parental home. The bride's mother prepares a feast of Bengali delicacies, including two or three different varieties of fish, puris, mishti bhaat (sweet rice, an all-time favourite), and lots of sweets like payash, rasgullas and gulab jamuns. This meal allows extended family and friends of the bride to express their good wishes and helps fortify her for the big wedding day.

Functions on the wedding day

Tamil Brahmins perform a ceremony just before the wedding called janavasam. Both sides assemble at a temple. The bride's parents offer the groom new clothes and then take him to the ceremony in an open car, along with a procession of both sides' wedding parties.

Punjabis (and some other Hindu north Indian groups) hold a special ceremony called the chooda. The chooda, or the red and white bangles that signify marital status, are put on the bride in a solemn ceremony. Traditionally the bride must wear them for at least 40 days after her wedding. Simultaneously, the boy's side has the sehra bandhi just before the groom gets on his horse. In this ceremony the groom's male relatives tie a floral veil (or sehra) over the groom's face, and then they all put on turbans. The sehra only comes off when the groom and the bride are face to face. His sisters bless the horse and feed it gram to bring a successful start to the wedding rituals. Then the baraat procession finds its way to the marriage venue.

Wedding traditions

In Christian weddings, the groom's brother is often the best man and carries the rings that the couple will exchange. And in all families, the groom's brother welcomes the bride into his family. According to Hindu belief, the wife of one's elder brother becomes a mother figure.

Real-life Wedding Belles:

Netra and Raghava, 8–10 July 2007, Bangalore

Netra and Raghava are a couple who don't lack creativity. She's a violinist and he's a popular artist. So for their wedding, with 5,000 guests—the event of the year in Bangalore—they combined their talents to display a new take on their janavasam.

The traditional south Indian procession usually happens in an old car. The couple arrived instead in a colourful auto rickshaw, with a masthead fully painted by Raghava—as a band played old-fashioned Tamil filmi music. A group of their friends, dressed in dhotis, pushed the auto from behind, while other friends and guests danced in front. The procession included a group of ladies carrying the seere (the traditional silver items for the couple's new house), traditional Tamil dancers performing the village tiger dance known as puliyattam, and a huge, synchronised fireworks display.

Netra requested only entertainment that was 'relevant and personal', so when the ensemble arrived at the hall, the couple's friends treated them to a dapankoothe, a raucous ethnic Tamil folk dance. Their closest pals had spent several weeks learning the dance!

The memorable event was a huge success. Netra described how special it was to have friends performing for her and Raghava, and to be able to infuse their passions and personality into their wedding. The janavasam let the couple show off 'the entire larger-than-life, mad, crazy, artistic side of the wedding to our guests,' she recalled.

Out of the box: Unusual pre-wedding party ideas

Do you and your fiancé dance to your own beat? It's your wedding and what better way to express yourselves than with an unconventional bash. As we interviewed brides, we discovered some fabulous ideas for pre-wedding parties that don't fit any prescribed formula.

Disco party

'We had a party which we called the Denim and Bling party which was, as the name suggests, very shiny! We had a dance floor with disco music by our friend Robby who is a part-time DJ, and strobe lights and everything. The party was at home and the food and drinks provided by Sharath and James. I'd definitely recommend them. Keep the snacks coming and don't bother too much about the main course. Just one or two dishes will suffice because everyone generally ends up getting trashed and the food will otherwise simply go to waste.'
— Nisha, Bangalore

Booze cruise

'My father-in-law threw a party on board a cruise, three days before the wedding. We called it the booze cruise, and it was quite different. We were sailing and there was everything from great food and great cocktails to a casino set up with fake money. The cruise was decorated with lights and it was awesome!'
— Sasha, Mumbai

Arabian night

'We had a youngster's party in Rambagh Palace, Jaipur, with DJ Aqueel, shishas and a Moroccan theme, and food by ITC at all functions. The boy's side arranged a very fun afternoon of elephant polo—a complete hit with everyone!'
— Suruchi, Bangalore

The Main Event

It's here—the big day you've probably been waiting for your whole life. Or one that your Significant Other sprung on you with a solitaire in your soup. However you see it, you know you want everything to run smoother than the icing on your three-tier reception cake.

In this chapter, we're going to discuss the elements that come together to make your big wedding day special. (Make sure you follow through to the next chapter, where we talk in more depth about the vendors who help put together a wedding, and how to best work with them to pull off your dream day.)

Wedding traditions

In some Punjabi families, the brother (with his wife if he's married) brings water from the nearby temple or the closest neighbour's house for the bride to bathe with after her haldi and chooda ceremony. In Bengali weddings, when the bride comes out upon her groom's arrival, she sits on a chowki and holds betel leaves over her eyes. Then her brothers, male cousins or friends lift her up so she can put the garland around her groom's neck.

The Ceremony

No matter what religion and cultural traditions you follow, this is the actual reason you've all come together, in celebratory mode. Details are specific to your priest, pandit, community and family, but here's our general advice on how to best approach the big event.

'I do' to-dos

Work out an event flow for the ceremony. Or better still, many different event flows. One for you, one for the groom, one for close relatives who are involved in the planning and one that you can print up as a programme to help guests get a clear idea of what's on the agenda.

The officiating priest

Family or older relatives from either the bride's or groom's side usually take care of finding the priest. Choose someone who's been officiating at all your family ceremonies for decades; or if not, a pandit who'll explain the rites in layman's language as he goes along. Availability is also an important factor, as the priest of your choice should be able to work on one of the auspicious days you've chosen. Going by all the brides we spoke to, this decision is a matter of custom, comfort levels or convenience. One couple, Neha and Gaurav from New Delhi, chose to be married by the bride's family pandit, while another bride, Shikha, let her groom's family in Delhi make arrangements (two officiating priests), as her folks were coming in from Lucknow and wouldn't have known whom to call in.

Getting it rite

Some brides simply love the rituals. While some others consider them a rite of passage that just has to be dealt with. Here are some tips on how to enjoy the ceremony:

First things first, have a clear idea of exactly what's going to happen throughout so that you don't land up fumbling, giggling or yawning through the ceremony. We may not follow the Western rehearsal dinner tradition in India, but getting a step-by-step run through of the rites will help you and your husband follow them better.

- Pay attention to what the priest is saying. It won't do to miss a step while daydreaming about your future! Also, it's special when you understand the significance of the ceremony.
- Make sure you've drunk water or visited the restroom before the rites. Check with a close family elder what to do if you just have to answer nature's call midway.
- Have a friend on standby to fetch and carry essentials and to leave your emergency kit with. You never know what may crop up. (See what to carry in it on p 100.)
- Remember that everyone's there to celebrate YOUR special day. This 'big picture' perspective will get you through the trauma of sitting still through it all, and then smiling non-stop through greeting and meeting a slew of relatives whose names you can't recall.

Real-life Wedding Belles Remember Their Interfaith Weddings

'My husband is Hindu and I am Catholic, so we got married by both rites. In the morning, we had a simple Hindu wedding, followed by lunch. The Catholic wedding was at 4 p.m. As my husband did not convert we missed many rites. We then proceeded to the reception hall.'—Archana, Mumbai

'My husband is Christian, I am Hindu-Muslim. We needed to incorporate an Arya Samaj wedding and also a Christian wedding blessing. My parents did a lot, as Samir and I lived in New York, and the wedding was in Goa. I wanted the Arya Samaj wedding at a small village, Velin, in Goa that my grandmother belonged to. We also did the Christian wedding blessing.' — Kavya, Goa

'I am a Marwari and my husband French. He would not have followed most of the customs anyway, nor would I. We had a legal wedding first followed by Arya Samaj rites. My in-laws knew nothing about our customs and we did not know about theirs. Everyone cooperated, and just enjoyed the differences.' — Shweta, Bangalore/St Mathurin sur Loire

'My husband's father is Zoroastrian, his mother Catholic; my parents are Sindhis and believe in the teachings of Guru Paramahansa Yogananda. We chose a spiritual wedding ceremony instead of a religious one. To bless our union, my MIL read from the Bible, my FIL read from the Avesta; my mother recited a poem about love by our Guruji, my father read from the Granth Sahib; my sister-in-law and her husband blessed us with a Jain prayer and a close family friend read a passage from the Koran. It made the experience very sacred and special.' — Arati, Bangalore

How to plan

If you and he come from similar backgrounds, identify a go-to person among the family elders and jot down the basic must-dos that you'll have to arrange for and how to go about them. In case both come from different cultures, it's imperative that you sit down and discuss which rites are right for you. One couple, Maharashtrian Janaki and Kashmiri Rahul, decided to enjoy the best of both worlds at their wedding. Janaki says, 'The wedding was held at the Leela Palace, Bangalore, and was predominantly Maharashtrian, but also included all the important Kashmiri wedding rites. The pandits for the wedding had come down from Pune. As we had combined both traditions, we created an informative booklet for all the guests explaining the importance of the ceremony and the significance of the rites.'

Keeping the guests in mind like that is thoughtful, but it's even more important to keep your immediate family, especially older members, in the loop so that they feel included rather than bewildered. For example, a south Indian family may not understand the concept of the north Indian milni where each member of the bride's family greets his or her counterpart in the baraat and ushers them into the wedding venue. Find out and explain the significance of all the 'alien' customs to the opposite side and give precise instructions on what to wear, do, and say, so that there's no confusion or bruised feelings later.

What to bring

You'll need a lot of different gear for your rites (ranging from flowers, ghee and incense at the Hindu vidhi mandap to the rings on a cushion for the Christian nuptials). Each religious denomination has a must-bring list that you can get from your officiating priest. Ask him to spell it out to you clearly, so that there's no last-minute running around.

The legalities

For Christians, Muslims, Parsis, Jews, and Bahai's, a marriage certificate issued by the religious authority is considered legal proof of the marriage. However, in the case of Hindus, Jains, Sikhs and Buddhists, the certificate issued by the religious organisation is not sufficient; hence they still need to obtain a formal marriage certificate from the registrar. A marriage certificate is essential for things like changing the bride's name on her passport and other documents, applying for a visa or ration card, etc. Instead of waiting until you really need it and wasting a lot of time, make the registration part of the wedding rituals. Many couples also opt for a simple civil marriage rather than all the elaborate functions of the religious marriage. It's a matter of personal choice.

How to register your marriage

Under the Special Marriage Act, 1954, a Notice of Intended Marriage has to be given in writing to the Marriage Officer of the district in which either you or your groom has lived for at least 30 days immediately preceding the date on which you give notice. This notice allows anyone who thinks that you are contravening any of the conditions of eligibility for a legal marriage to object. After 30 days, provided no one objects, you visit the Marriage Officer along with three witnesses to solemnise your marriage.

How to add pizzazz to a registered wedding

No one said a registered wedding has to just be a boring, signing-on-the-dotted-line kind of affair. There are ways to make this memorable, as one couple, Maya and Abodh, did, when they had their nearest and dearest around them as they signed the register in Mumbai. Says Maya, 'It was quite a lot of fun. We sat on those ornate wedding chairs that are placed on a stage right behind where you sign. They look completely surreal in the very government office environment. And after the 'ceremony', we went outside to the steps of the Asiatic Library nearby and a close friend who's a professional photographer did an impromptu photo shoot that turned out great!' There are innumerable ways to add

zing to the registering: whether it's enjoying the inherent irony in the kitschy chairs, posing for wedding photos, arranging for a low-key musical instrument just outside the registry office, or even setting free a gigantic bunch of helium-filled balloons to mark the event.

Great br-ideas: Our favourite wedding ceremony themes

Wondering what sort of wedding scene to choose? If the décor is for your wedding ceremony, here are some options:

* Opulent: Lots of gilded baroque columns and maroon velvet upholstery. Think massive strings of marigolds interspersed with golden balls, and ornate thrones for you and your groom. Think a traditional wedding straight out of 1970s Bollywood.

* Simple yet traditional: Fresh flowers and your community-specific décor all the way. For example, a backdrop with Kutchhi mirror work or a wooden jharokha to suit a Gujarati wedding or lovely brass lamps for the Kerala touch.

* Contemporary: Mediterranean-style clean lines and Swedish wooden or stainless steel furniture sitting cheek by jowl with all the ceremonial paraphernalia.

* New age: Jewel-toned raw silk, incense, kitschy or ironic things like love seats or painted trunks for your guests to sit on.

* Beach: Shell-encrusted décor and gauzy white curtains around the shamiana you'll erect so that guests get the shade as well as the balmy breeze.

The Venue for the Rites and Reception

Muslims and Hindus can have their rites anywhere—a place of worship, home, hotel or marriage hall—as long as a maulvi or pandit officiates. If you're Hindu, you'll need to check whether your venue allows for the havan fire. The Sikh ceremony, called anand karaj (rite of happiness), is conducted inside a gurdwara. Christian weddings in India mostly occur in a church, although some couples who opt for an exchange of vows elsewhere, like a Goan beach. Syrian Christians, however, have a more elaborate wedding service in a church. Parsis need to have a fire temple close at hand, and most rites are performed within the agyaari premises.

You'll also need to factor in whether you want to have your reception on the same day at the same venue. In Punjabi weddings, the merrymaking reception comes first, segueing into the solemn pheras that are done late into the night. In this case you'd want to choose a place that could segue accordingly!

So basically, your ceremony venue will depend on your religion, denomination, community, budget and even personal attachment. Like Kavya from Bangalore, who was keen to tie the knot with her groom Samir, at the family temple in the Velin village of old Goa, where her paternal grandma came from. 'Generations of my family have worshipped there and I was very sure that I wanted my Arya Samaj ceremony there,' she recounts.

In the traditional set-up, the reception party is hosted by the groom's side, but in more contemporary weddings, it's often the bride and groom who spend the money and take decisions. It's really up to you whether you want to have one venue for both the rites as well as the reception, or different ones for each.

In the air, under water, online—you can let your imagination take charge as long as you have super planning skills for the extra craziness involved!

Types of venues

* Religious: Temples, churches, gurdwaras, Parsi fire temples, etc., as well as their grounds, are ideal places to have the ceremony and even post-wedding party.

* Commercial: Hotels, wedding halls, pandals, houses for hire, even school or college playgrounds.

* Unusual: Beaches, forests, palaces; actress Raveena Tandon married Anil Thadani in the Jag Mandir Palace in Udaipur, Rajasthan. Mountaineering enthusiasts Ashirwad and Bharti made the newspapers when they took their wedding vows 2,000 feet above ground in February 2005, suspended midair on ropes in mountains off Lonavala. The priest chanted the wedding mantras suspended on a rope too, with just a quick, 30 minutes of training! Another couple, Sunil and Vandana, had their rites in a hot-air balloon floating above Jaipur, in December 2006.

Setting the stage: Stage decorations and flowers

These are the elements that will bring your fantasy wedding to life. Choosing the right decorations is central to creating a wedding that is truly 'you'. You don't want someone who offers you OTT Bollywood extravaganza when you're dreaming of understated Victorian elegance.

Sets

Earlier, a wedding set was not much more than a decorated, maroon-and-gold stage and lots of colourful pandals or marquees with makeshift furniture. All this could be set up within a few hours. But the modern-day wedding can be quite a production. Sets can be really elaborate and unique or surprisingly simple—options abound. With unlimited materials and money at your disposal, you could create just about any look that you want to go with your theme, from a fairy-tale castle to a Hawaiian beach. What you settle on will largely be dictated by your inclination, your imagination and your budget.

Stage

The traditional stage setting is about two or three feet off the ground, festooned with marigolds, covered by a maroon carpet and bearing twin 'thrones' for you and your groom to sit on. A trendier option today is to have a joint love seat instead of two separate chairs with armrests. The bride's and groom's seating is usually flanked by a few less elaborate seats for parents, siblings, young cousins or close friends to sit on by turn, as they help stow away gifts and flowers you receive. The backdrop usually bears strings of flowers, intricate floral designs, drapes or even kitschy red hearts with your names inscribed on them. But with couples getting increasingly design savvy these days, it's not uncommon to find unusual colours, themes and more modern stage furniture. Explore your options or even custom-design what you have in mind.

Flowers

It's just not an Indian wedding without flowers. Fresh, dewy ones. In copious quantities. To festoon the entrance, the foyer or greeting area, the stage, as centrepieces for individual and buffet tables both. And many brides are carrying a posy of flowers at their reception. (Partly, we suspect, so they can toss the bouquet at their single friends later!)

Lighting

Stringing metres of little lights through trees and bushes for an open-air venue or lighting lamps in an indoor one are inexpensive and easy ways to add a magical touch to the evening. In lighting, as in all elements of the décor, less is usually more. Especially if the weather isn't very cool to begin with—remember that bulbs also emit heat along with the light. And if you're using halogen lights for the stage, ensure that your eyes and make-up can stand the strain of being under harsh light for two to four hours. Also make sure the stage lighting flatters your make-up, clothes and skin to best effect so that you look absolutely fab in person as well as in your wedding pictures.

Great br-ideas to splurge or save on

Splurge: The sky's the limit. If you want to go the way of US-based millionaire hotelier Vikram Chatwal and model Priya Sachdev who married in 2006, order your decorations from every corner of the earth—50,000 kilos of flowers from Holland, Bangkok, and Kolkata, burn 3,000 candles and use 65,000 metres of fabric.

Save: Stages are getting increasingly passé, so opt to informally mingle with your guests instead. This will save you considerable expense, too. Get a creatively inclined friend to help out with 50–75 pretty table centrepieces if you don't have a mammoth guest list. Or try floating tealights in coloured glasses, traditional diyas or single flowers on tables, or cheery lanterns strung around the venue.

Fabulous flowers

Types of flowers can range from the auspicious and traditional marigold to the exotic orchid or anthurium. For striking arrangements for your buffet or table centrepieces, consider these décor tricks and trends:

Colour and texture. Go for a monochromatic arrangement of all the same type of flower (who doesn't love a vase of pink roses?), or vary one factor (a variety of different pink flowers or all roses but in different hues), or have a mix of blooms in a palette of coordinating colours.

Height and numbers For centrepieces, you want to choose a short, tight arrangement, or something in a tall clear vase that doesn't block guests from easily talking with each other. Mix and match with short blooms at some tables and taller ones at others Or replace the traditional one vase per table with a grouping of smaller bud vases, all clustered together as one arrangement.

Candles. Candlelight does wonders for the mood of your event. Set up a circle of votives around your flowers, or work with your decorator to come up with other ways to incorporate candles.

Water. Float a gardenia blossom in a shallow bowl (maybe with candles, too), or submerge a long stem of orchids under water filling a tall vase. For a different effect, colour your water.

Creative containers. Think outside of the conventional glass bowl and use baskets, urns, or pots in silver, ceramic or terracotta. Family heirlooms, jewellery boxes or teapots make great flower holders, too. Remember, not every table has to match.

Uncut. Plants are a great alternative to cut arrangements. Some pots can give a casual feel, or use sculpted topiaries or miniature trees for a polished look.

Other elements. Twigs, berries, rocks or coloured glass add character to any arrangement. Or for a burst of colour, intersperse flowers with green apples or cut lemons, limes or oranges.

Guest seating

This will depend on the activities planned and the way the food is going to be served. Some couples have rows of chairs facing the stage in one large hall, while the food is served in another section. This demarcates the formal greeting-and-congratulating-the-couple-onstage part of the evening from the rest of the festivities. It's important to make the seating for lunch or dinner comfortable. The traditional way is to either have floor seating or long rows of tables with chairs placed along one side, so waiters can serve the guests nicely. This is still adhered to at Parsi weddings, where the serving of the lagan nu bhonu is as finely tuned as an operatic operation. Or if you don't want everyone to be eating en masse, an elegant yet less formal seating plan would be to have round tables laid out with dining service all through the venue. That way, people are free to sit where they choose and visit the buffet tables as often as they like. If you prefer a formal sit-down dinner (although a word of warning: this doesn't quite work in our country, thanks to our Stretchable Standard Time and difficulties with the concept of the RSVP), you'll need to work out a seating chart and arrange for place cards with everyone's names on them. This could also give rise to a fair amount of awkwardness if your uncle's wife's sister-in-law's father decides to bring along five of his closest friends (as is quite common in large weddings) and is horrified to find that their names are not mentioned anywhere! So, only try this if you're sure of a small, intimate and manageable gathering at your wedding day celebratory meal.

Paper work

A guest book at the entrance lets your guests leave their words of wisdom and wishes. It also allows you to guess how many people were at your wedding. (And this will help when you're trying to figure out, with the caterer, how many guests enjoyed the meal—to be added to your bill!) Programmes explaining the event flow are now all the rage, and double as keepsakes/thank you cards for all the guests. You can also consider seating cards (for small parties with assigned seating).

Our favourite wedding reception themes

You can be as imaginative as you want with the theme of your reception or just simply go classic. Here are some of our favourite reception themes:

- Arty Indian: Prints of plush paintings by your favourite contemporary Indian artists, highlighted with strategic lighting, around the venue. Or fill the entire wall behind your stage with a blown-up Rajasthani miniature, or an eye-catching mural in a wedding theme. Earthenware jars with Warli or Madhubani paintings on them, topped with wooden or marble roundels can make interesting centre tables for your guests to lounge around.
- Graeco-Roman: Elegant columns, giant amphorae filled with fresh flowers, ornate lounge chairs—they'll all complement the graceful clothes and beautiful jewellery that you can sport to go with this theme.
- British garden: You could have your reception party at 4 p.m. on a Sunday to show off your dusky rose fusion-lehenga in the golden sunlight. Wicker furniture on a lush lawn and flower arbours to provide shade will make a pretty picture.
- Turkish evil eye: 'Nazar' is something so ingrained in our psyche, that your older guests will identify with this theme, while the younger ones will appreciate it for its exotic appeal. And the deep blue of the Turkish evil eye amulets is a very attractive colour. Have it on your outfit, put the concentric circles on table tops, on lanterns, or as the backdrop on the stage.
- Southeast Asian: Mood lighting, lotus-filled pools of water, gleaming brassware, serene Buddhas and other statuary, an earthy-yet-rich feel with lots of wood, plants and natural materials, etc.

Ask the experts

We asked Nitinn Raichooda, director of Perfect Décor in Mumbai and of wedding decorators.com, to give us the scoop on what's hot on the wedding décor front.

Which is the most popular colour scheme today?
Silver and turquoise blue for receptions.

What are the factors that help a couple choose their wedding theme and colour?
* Budget is the most important factor.
* These days, couples like to explore different sources like the internet, magazines, wedding exhibitions and wedding specials in newspapers for guidance.
* Brides like to match the décor to the colour and style of their wedding dress or ensemble.

Does this vary from city to city? If yes, how?
Yes, it DOES vary from city to city. The best designs and creative work come from the major metros, particularly Mumbai, Jaipur, Chandigarh, Delhi, Hyderabad.

What is the minimum amount that a bride should budget for basic flowers at her reception?
This depends on the venue (closed or open lawns), the weather, and the décor style chosen. It starts at about Rs 40,000 and spirals upwards. Many couples, or even the parents of the bride and groom, set themselves a budget and then soon go over it as they start seeing what's on offer.

What innovations in floral arrangements are popular these days?
The use of exotic flowers like liliums, carnations, chrysanthemums, coloured orchids, anthuriums, etc., in stylish arrangements with special light effects, is gaining popularity over the traditional marigolds.

Catering

For the majority of guests at an elaborate Indian wedding, the most memorable details are the ones that are associated with the loaded buffet tables! Often, the success of a reception (or any other wedding revelry), is gauged by how tasty, varied and plentiful the food is.

The right caterer is of the essence. A caterer not only helps you select a suitable menu, s/he also manages a team of chefs, kitchen hands, stewards and other wait staff; and often provides crockery, cutlery, glassware, linen and, in some cases, table dressings.

Let's explore each of the elements in detail.

Menu

The caterer usually offers some sample menus you can pick from, and then add or subtract dishes from, according to your preferences. The basic items for any wedding meal will include: refreshments and snacks served on platters at the start of the reception, starters, soup/salad, main course, side dishes, breads, fruit, desserts, coffee, paan, etc. Although multiple cuisine kiosks and live pasta corners have been almost mandatory at weddings for the last decade or so, there's now a move towards quality versus ostentation. So, you can go for a tasteful gourmet menu that has everything from imported fish and cheese to exotic desserts, instead of the usual tandoori-Mughlai-Chinese-Italian-Lebanese-chaat tamasha.

You might want to pick a menu and style of service that suits your group's traditions or blends them with the modern. For example, Mumbai's famous caterer of Parsi lagan nu bhonu, Tanaz Godiwala, now offers a variation of the traditional paatra ni machhi. The original, which was a chutney-filled leaf-wrapped pomfret steamed to perfection, can now be a quintet of succulent prawns doused in the same green sauce and similarly steamed and served. Or there's the Bohri community's wedding meal, normally served in large thaalis or plates that four or five people sit around and eat from together. This meal, which starts with a large serving of dessert, is now being redefined thanks to calorie-counting wedding guests; the dessert going from traditional falooda-kulfi or ice cream, to sugar-free, fat-free gelato!

Great br-ideas to save on

You can get creative by getting a chaat, pav-bhaji or dosa street vendor to set up his stall at the venue and prepare scrumptious, fresh savouries for all your guests on the spot. Add a bit of fun by creating a mela ambience—bring in a jalebi maker, fortune teller, portrait artist, bangle vendor and mehendi artist. All these vendors won't charge a lot, but they will add some rustic charm to your simple celebration. A more sophisticated yet relatively inexpensive alternative is to invite your guests to a formal, post-ceremony high tea. This way, you can serve only finger food like canapés and homemade hors d'oeuvres with tea, juice or wine. Cucumber sandwiches may sound really elegant, but are actually very economical and easy to make.

Basic traditional menu (north Indian)

Starters

Stuffed mushroom and capsicum
Variety of chaats including aloo tikki
Variety of veg and non-veg kebabs and tikkas

Entrée

Paneer palak/Butter chicken
Mix veg korma
Dal makhani/Maa ki dal
Pulao and dum biryani (veg/non-veg)
Variety of naans

Sides

Salad, raita, chutneys, pickles and papad

Desserts

Rasmalai
Gajar ka halwa/Gulab jamuns
Vanilla ice cream with chocolate sauce

Afters

Paans, mouth fresheners, tea/coffee

Adding the contemporary touch

* Have a healthy salad counter and make the starters bite-sized.
* Go fusion: a dab of wasabi sauce on steamed rawas or Mediterraneanstyle-veggies.
* Serve on stylish conduction counters instead of the standard covered dishes.

Setting the table

Crockery, cutlery and glassware

This is one of the extras that the caterer may or may not provide. But it's best to check who is offering what, way in advance. If your caterer doesn't do these, you might have to check with the decorator or the venue to see if they can. Quality and quantity depends on your budget and number of guests, and cleanliness is of paramount importance. The types and sizes of plates and spoons required will also depend on your menu (no soup spoons unless you're serving soup, right?). These days, sit-down brunches, lunches, or dinners for select guests are quite the happening option. In this case, it's fashionable to use exclusive face plates or ornate dishes as base plates over which various other plates for each course are placed. Glassware, too, depends on what drinks you're serving.

Napiery and table dressings: Napkins, tablecloths, centrepieces

Again, this is one of the extras that the caterer may or may not provide. Spotless table linen and nicely folded napkins at each place setting create a great first impression, and begin your guests' dining experience nicely. Sometimes, a caterer can provide decorative centrepieces (so you wouldn't have to get this from a decorator); an exhibition table of carved fruits and vegetables, baked sculptures or ice sculptures, for example.

Great br-ideas to splurge on

People's palates are being exposed to so many global influences—there's nothing to stop you from getting ambitious about the menu at your big fat Indian wedding. Fly in exotic fare from across the world or go for home-grown five-star catering. One sure-fire impression maker is personalising something—say, individual dessert cakes with your names entwined in the icing—or a take-home goodie bag for each guest with sugared almonds, a teeny bottle of extra virgin olive oil and/or a packet of Gruyere cheese for them to enjoy later and remember you fondly.

Photography and video

You'll preserve your special day for posterity with stills and videos. Capture those special moments—the private smile you and your man share, the laughter and light moments with your siblings, the look in your parents' eyes. If you're lucky, like Nisha who married Sidharth in Delhi in December 2005, you'll find a team which makes this seem effortless. Says Nisha, 'My in-laws picked Baadal Jain, whose team really knows how to deal with brides! He arranged the posing and asked me to smile and look this way or that and I just followed. I landed up enjoying it actually.'

The photographers and video crew will offer you a variety of options in terms of photo print sizes, finishes (matte or glossy), special effects, albums, video cassettes, CDs, DVDs and online publication of your wedding pictures. And what sort of memories do you want to create? Classic? Candid? Kitschy? Crazy? Take your pick. Atul Joshi, whose team of cameramen has been shooting weddings in and around Mumbai for almost a decade, says, 'It's important to convey to your photographer what kind of images you want. Most people like the tried-and-tested posed shots with miles of smiles and every hair in place. But a lot of younger, more independent-minded couples are also opting for realistic or journalistic pictures—grainy black-and-whites, candid shots, behind-the-scenes images, etc.' A mix of posed shots plus realistic candids can come together to tell the story of your wedding day.

Great br-ideas: Getting a video that complements your photography

Ask your video team to choose a nice vantage point from where they can get footage of the interesting events that the still cams can't capture well. Guests entering the venue and being greeted by your family, the action on the dance floor, the little kids racing around, your sister checking out the groom's handsome cousin, the kitchen staff adding the garnish to platters—all the details that will bring back your wedding day to you in technicolour decades later.

Great br-ideas to splurge or save on

Splurge: Have a couple of guys with Polaroid cameras doing copious amounts of instant pictures that the guests can take home with them. This will make your guests feel really special and you'll be able to capture a lot of impromptu memorable moments (provided your family members and friends remember to scan their Polaroids and post them to the same website you're using!).

Save: Instead of hiring the entire camera outfit from the time you're getting dressed until your last guest leaves, ask them to come in at a designated time and shoot pictures of just you and your closest family members and friends. Or delegate digicams to friends you know will enjoy recording the evening, and make sure you email pictures to everyone or post them on a common website so guests can save them. This way, you can keep your vendor costs to a minimum without wasting valuable album space on your great-aunt's best friend, without offending anyone.

Wedding traditions

The bride's maternal uncles play a role in Andhra Vaishnava weddings, carrying the bride to the kalyana mandapam (marriage hall), with the ladies of the household following in a procession. They seat the bride opposite the groom, but with a curtain in between them so they won't see each other until the shubha muhurtham (auspicious time for the marriage rites). The bride's and groom's respective maternal uncles lift the couple, in a Tamil Shaivite community marriage. Then, while the bride and groom are up on their family's shoulders, they garland each other three times to complete their union!

Giving and Receiving Gifts

It wouldn't be a wedding without the presents! The gifts will actually start rolling in as soon as you and your groom decide to tie the knot. Getting gifts is fab, of course (it's like your birthday ten times over!), but it's a little tricky as well, because you'll want to respond, with perfect etiquette, to anyone who takes the time to gift you something. And you and your family will have to choose just the right gifts for the groom's side as well, which can be a tricky business, even while fun and satisfying.

Great br-ideas

If you don't want any gifts, or you'd rather they make a donation to your favourite charity in lieu of presents, mention it discreetly on your wedding invitation

Presents of mind: Handling wedding gifts

Most of your family and friends will buy you gifts without asking what you want or need. Some wedding guests will slip cash into an envelope—which is actually great. Gold, in the form of coins, rings, etc. is a common gift, but some of the brides we spoke to preferred more personal gifts, like cocktail glasses or books of poetry.

Your nearest and dearest may know your likes well enough to shop for you, but other guests may end up giving you crystal vases when you hate glass, or silver bowls that you already have three dozen of. One young bride who is a graduate of NID was not so excited when someone gave her a feng shui fountain she didn't take to. If you're lucky, some guests will ask for gift ideas. If you feel comfortable, it's fine to let them know what would tickle your fancy, says etiquette expert Rukshana Eisha of Image Inc. 'If the enquiries are from close friends and relatives, then it is acceptable to tell them what you would like. Try not to be too extravagant though with your demands,' Eisha advises.

Make a wish-list in different price ranges, probably with your fiancé. Post it on your wedding website, and share it with your parents and in-laws-to-be as well—just in case they get asked on your behalf. Gift registries at home décor or department stores make the gift-buying process simple for guests (who want to buy the couple something they want without much effort) and for the couple (who want to receive items they like and need for

Great br-ideas for gift givers

Think ahead about whether or not it's appropriate to bring your gift to the wedding ceremony or reception. Gifting flowers isn't the best idea at the wedding, for example, as there will be dozens of bouquets there already. And what will happen to your arrangement after the event, who will cart it home? The same philosophy applies to heavy gift boxes, which will be cumbersome to carry back. Have them delivered, instead, to the bride's residence or her new home.

Ask the experts: What do I register for?

Good Earth's bridal consultants suggest asking for the following items:

* Formal dining service for 12 in bone china

* Daily dining ware

* Tea service for 12. Complete the look with linen cocktail napkins!

*Cutlery for 12

* Stylish drinking glasses.

* Wine glasses, Eisch and Riedel are some really good brands. For a less traditional alternative, try versions in coloured brown glass. And Riedel's crystal duck-shaped decanter makes for a great bar accent as well.

* A silver-plated ice bucket, tongs and salver

* High quality towels in luxurious white and cream micro-cotton

* 300 thread count bed linen and duvet

* Home décor: a candelabra with crystals, a silver plated vase, or a selection of clear glass vases

their home). Gift registries are not yet popular in India. Frazer and Haws giftware stores, which have outlets in Delhi and Bangalore, will keep a couple's wish-list on file, and then tick purchased items off so another guest doesn't buy you a duplicate. And the Good Earth home décor stores in Mumbai and Delhi have a bridal wish-list programme and bridal consultants to help engaged couples. It also offers worldwide delivery, customised table ware stamped with your wedding date, gift wrapping, and a weekly email update that lists which items have been bought so far, which are close to being out of stock (in case a bride wants to buy them herself) and suggestions for new things the bride may want to add to her wish-list.

Real-life Wedding Belles
Remember Their Gift Favourites and Duds

Favourites:

'Definitely my husband and a very handy coffee maker.' — Payal, Kolkata

'The cocktail glasses and photo frames.' — Latha, Andhra Pradesh

'A beautiful diamond mangalsutra gifted by my husband.' — Nupur, Delhi

'A pair of stuffed toys—one purple elephant with pink ears and Winnie the Pooh.' — Sasha, Mumbai

'The best wedding gift I received was a beautiful set of lamps.' — Archana, Mumbai

'A collection of old John Donne leatherbound books for my library.' — Suruchi, Bangalore

'Thangam Philip's cookbooks (in English) were the best.' — Suzanna, Bangalore

'The best were bed linen sets because they were functional yet chic.' — Karlette, Delhi

Duds

'A gaudy and flashy bedspread.' — A Bangalore bride

'A sari that was out of fashion.' — A Delhi bride

'Tacky and tasteless gold ornaments.' — A Jaipur bride

'A decoration piece with the price tag left on.' — A Delhi bride

'The worst—some wooden spoons, casserole, and many more!' — A Delhi bride

'I guess the numerous wall clocks that I got would qualify for the worst because they are just too common.' — A Mumbai bride

'Tis better to give than to receive: Gifts from the bride and her family

Though dowry is illegal, it's now common for both sides to exchange gifts, a custom that allows the two sides to welcome and honour their counterparts as they come together into one bigger family.

So like many modern brides, you and your family will probably be buying gifts for your in-laws, and receiving gifts back from them. The custom of gift exchanges doesn't change per religion, but almost every family does it differently. Some during the sagan ceremony, others during roka or engagement. The groom's side traditionally brings at least one set of clothes and jewellery for the bride, and each family has its own traditional bridal gifts, such as green or red glass bangles, sindoor (vermilion), fruits, sweetmeats, etc. Muslims also gift henna for the bridal mehendi party.The bride's side then reciprocates. Some Hindu maternal uncles help provide gifts for the groom's family, as part of a bhaat gift to the bride's mother to pass on later to the groom's family.

There are customary gifts for the groom including the wedding outfit, shoes, watch or jewellery gifted by your family, plus you might want to gift a truly personal and special gift to your husband after marriage. It could be the new laptop he didn't get because he spent his savings on your engagement ring. Or a fancy designer money clip you think he'd like to use. Even a piece of jewellery.

And then how should you decide what to buy the various members of the groom's side? Eisha advises purchasing 'something personal or something of value that can be kept over the years also as a remembrance of the occasion'. Think about their lifestyle and preferences. It makes sense to check if your husband's sister who lives in Australia would wear a heavy silk sari there, or whether a pair of elegant gold earrings would be more useful to her. Ask around the family to find out what each member would like, or just ask your recipients directly. You could even take them out shopping with you—but do be careful when setting expectations so your giftee doesn't choose something that's more expensive than what you have in mind.

For a smooth gift-buying process, follow our tips:

- List the members of the groom's family you need to buy gifts for.
- Get advice from the groom about his family's tastes and customs.
- Try traditional gift choices if you're at a loss, or if you have too long a list: cash, gold jewellery, seasonal clothing, or other accessories (like watches for the male relatives of the groom). If you're looking for a more modern choice, consider a designer bag or a set of cocktail glasses, if you're sure of the recipient's taste.
- Wrap your gifts and personalise them, with a note. If you're hiring a trousseau packer, ask him or her to help with fancy packaging.

It's also common practise for the bride to give gifts to her own family and close friends. Some traditions demand that all the sisters and aunts get a sari or a little piece of jewellery. The amount you spend will depend on how closely you're related, or how strong your relationship with the person is. This is a hierarchy that's very personal, so be tactful to not step on any carefully pedicured toes. However, you may decide to sidestep tradition for a few special people and give presents that are more personal.

Wedding traditions

In a Bengali family, the mother-in-law welcomes the new bride home by offering her a fish to hold (traditionally a live fish!), while she waits for the milk to boil over (symbolising a house overflowing with food and affection). The bride then steps onto a platter containing alta (vermilion water) and walks into her new home, leaving the imprints of her feet on the floor of the house. Lastly, she is taken into the kitchen and blessed by all the elders.

Behind the Scenes

Working with Your Vendors

In the previous chapters, we've introduced you to all the vendors who will put the various bits of your wedding together and shape your events based on your vision and their experience. In this section, we give you practical ways to get the best out of all the commercial help involved in the wedding. You don't need a degree in people management for this, but considering the sheer number and diverse types of vendors you'll be dealing with, it might help to be organised and think things through in advance. That's where we come in.

First off, do your homework. Ask your friends and acquaintances for their vendor recommendations (since that's how most information travels in India). Make it a point to attend as many weddings as you can, and think back to what you liked about the functions you've been to. Hit up recently married couples for their favourite vendors' details. You can also find vendors through a wedding planner (if you're using one), and in magazines, the Yellow Pages or online.

If you haven't seen a vendor's work in person, ask to see photos, to have a peek at a project they're currently working on, or (for caterers or chocolate makers) for a tasting to ensure quality and consistency.

Keep a budget in mind, shop around to get the best deal and put your bargaining skills to work. Don't worry about looking cheap—vendors will respect you more if you get a good deal out of them! One negotiating tip: consider booking the same vendor for your pre-wedding functions, too, and you could benefit from discounts, as well as familiarity.

The vendor interview

We highly recommend an in-person interview with any of your top contenders. You wouldn't commit to any relationship without a first date, right? Here are some sample questions to help determine if you and the vendor are a good match:

* Do you do _____ (type of wedding based on style, community or religion) weddings?

* Would you be able to handle my wedding which is fixed for ____(date) with a guest list of ____ (number) invitees?

* What is your USP? Do you have any special deals/services/skills? What can you offer me that others can't?

* If I hire you to do my stationery, walk me through what happens between now and my wedding day.

* Do you have a back-up plan in case someone falls sick or something crucial goes wrong?

* What are your rates and preferred payment schedule?

* Can you work with my budget of Rs ________?

* Are you ready to work in my special requests?

* Do you provide a contract for your services that we both sign (and can I see it at this time)?

* Do you require a deposit?

* What are your cancellation policies? Can I get my deposit back?

* How many weddings have you handled? Can I have a couple of references?

Sealing the deal

Found the one? Chances are you won't be the only bride that's decided this vendor is appealing. To avoid the disappointment of finding the vendor booked up on your wedding date, come to an agreement as soon as you can make the decision. It's best to sign a written contract with your vendor to confirm deliverables, due dates, rates, payment schedule, and cancellation and refund policies. 'Unforeseen expenses' can crop up if you leave the agreement open-ended. Or in the event that your vendor doesn't provide a formal agreement, carry a pro forma letter into which you can fill in all the details of your booking, and make sure you and the venue owner/manager both sign. This may not be legally binding, but can act as a deterrent to someone likely to renege or goof up. Don't let the vendor sweet talk you or pretend s/he's too busy to formalise the agreement between you! Most vendors will ask you to pay a percentage of the rate that you agreed on in advance. Ask for a receipt for the same.

Tips for working with your vendor

- Think of the wedding ceremony or reception party as a Bollywood movie set. You need to set up the backdrop, the atmosphere and the props before the actors move in (you know who the hero and heroine are!). Your vendors have the expertise and the ideas. So, blindly trust them with your decisions. Nah! We're just kidding. Trust your vendors, but never defer to their tastes if you feel strongly, be it for or against. After all, it's your wedding, and you need to be happy with the end results!
- The key to an angst-free working relationship: clear briefs from you on your vision for each element, and detailed plans from your vendors so you know exactly what s/he is going to do by which milestone dates. For example, for your wedding stationery, have your designer or printer set dates by which you must select your designs, see the proofs, approve the proofs, and when the invitations will go out to the approved guest list. For vendors where you may be working with many people, ask for a one-point contact to answer

all your questions and make the necessary arrangements. Preferably this person will be present on your actual wedding day as well to make sure things go smoothly.

- Make sure your vendors have details of all events. For any item being delivered, like the boxes of chocolate you're giving out as favour to your sangeet guests, give clear instructions about the date, time, address and contact person the vendor must deliver to. And for vendors meeting you to perform their services at your party venue, like mehendi artists, DJs and photographers, make sure they have the address, contact details and exact directions. You don't want to be waiting around stressed while your mehendi team can't find their way to your party.
- Delegate on the big day—you're going to be frantically busy so ask a trusted friend or family member to be your vendor's point of contact throughout the wedding. Leave your vendor with a clear understanding of your requirements, and then have your surrogate check on the execution.
- If something isn't as you'd envisaged it, look at it calmly and practically, and decide whether it makes a big difference to your function. If you think it's crucial and just HAS to be changed, let your friend or family member take care of it. If not, let it pass... most guests will hardly notice tiny details, as they're here to see YOU.

Wedding traditions

In a Parsi wedding, the groom gives gifts to the sisters of the bride to buy his way out of a few rituals, including haath boravanu—where the groom cannot remove his hand from water until he pays money to the sisters; pag dhovanu—where the groom is threatened with milk on his shoes; and chero chorvanu—in which the seven strands of thread tying the couple together are removed upon payment.

Hitting the Spot: The Venue

The venue is where you will hold different functions of your wedding. It's important to pair each event with a venue that suits it in terms of size and style. You first need to shortlist the kind of venue you want (see p 52 for this). Then, while you're weighing the pros and cons of nani's farm versus a Goa beach house, consult our interview checklist.

When to book

Look for your venue five months before your wedding or as soon as you know your wedding date. For some brides getting the right venue is so important that they choose their date based on when their favourite venue is available.

Plan B? Very important! Check if there's a smaller hall close to the chosen venue that you could hire at a pinch. Else play safe and keep your home or a friend's large home on standby—if it's large enough—no one minds a bit of a crush if they're having fun!

The venue interview

* What kind of space do you have? How much of this is outdoors and how much indoors?
* Does the venue have all the facilities the ceremony requires? For example, permission and place for a havan for the Hindu pheras (especially as some venues, indoor ones at least, may have fire hazard issues), or a choir or sound system for the hymns in a Catholic wedding?
* Does the venue have temperature control (cooling in summer and heating in extreme winter)?
* Do you have more than one wedding going on at the same time?
* Can I work with my own decorators, florists, caterers and DJs, or do I have to hire someone you're affiliated with?
* Does the venue provide basic behind-the-scenes facilities like a dressing room, clean restrooms, mirrors, storage facility for valuables, parking, etc.?

What it costs

Rates vary widely. Most venues will ask you for an advance between 20% to half the amount.

Working with your venue

Here are some venue fundas to help you out.

Hygiene: Has everything (including the spare loo) been cleaned well?

Fittings: Ensure that all the plug points and electrical connections, water sources, flush tanks, door and window latches and locks, elevators, and anything else you'll be using, work. A small thing like a dead plug point may mean your stylist is not able to use a blow dryer for that last-minute touch up you sorely need after the drive to the venue on the big day. If you have a live band playing in an outdoor amphitheatre, are there enough plug points for them? Can the venue electrical system even take the load of their equipment?

Staff: You may want to meet the people who will be around to ensure that they understand what kind of wedding you're planning and also to see whether they're as presentable as you'd like them to be. You could always do something about their attire, if need be.

What's available and included: Does the hall have the right number of chairs and tables already there? Do they also provide table linen in a choice of colours? Make sure you check out all of the furniture and other elements you're planning to use.

Visualisation: Imagine what the venue will look like once it's done. Where do you want the seating? Where should the meal be served? Give your input on things such as how large you'd like your stage to be, how many seats to a table, or where the bar can be placed so your drinking friends can be close to your dancing buddies at the reception.

Confirmation: Check and recheck your booking. It's better to be paranoid than sorry. It doesn't happen often, but sometimes a venue double books by accident. Also, check to ensure that a noisy concert or event isn't being organised next door to your wedding.

Decoration: Once your people get started on the décor, keep a close check to see if your plans needs to be tweaked to suit the venue's requirements and limitations.

Setting the stage: Decorators and florists

The decorator and florist will create the look of your wedding by using decorations—floral and otherwise—and adding the right furniture and fittings.

When to book

Five months before the wedding, or as soon as you have a date and a venue.

What it costs

Costs vary. For the best deal, negotiate on the components of the decor (the stage, the chairs etc.) rather than the total.

The decorator/florist interview

* What kind of ideas do you have for the entrance, stage, and overall look of the venue?
* What materials do you use and can I see a few pictures of your designs or samples?
* How soon can you come up with a custom-made theme design for me?

Working with your decorator

There are various points when you (or those close to you) should check in on the decorator:

- At the sourcing stage. Ask to see samples of anything that your decorator is having custom-made before they go into production.
- At the set creation stage. Ask to see swatches of any fabric or paint that will be applied.
- At the hiring stage. If they're renting most of the things, you might want to accompany the decorator to the place where s/he's hiring most of the items from to make sure they suit your style mantra. Make sure they're planning to hire enough people to set up the decorations/flowers with time to spare (in case you need to make last-minute changes).
- At the halfway mark. When all the basics are in place and the detailing is still to be done. If you don't like the placements, you can make changes now.
- Once the flowers come in. These have to be fresh, so they have to come in just before the function. In case of marigolds and tuberoses, they can be strung up several hours ahead of time. But the later this is done, the fresher your party will feel. By this time you're going to be busy beautifying yourself, but send a family member to oversee this.
- At the 99% done stage. When all that's remaining is to roll out the carpets (this is usually done last to prevent stains) and switch on the lights.

Flowers checklist

* Which flowers do you want? In what hue do you want them?
* Find out how much the decorator or florist is going to charge you. Is it per flower, per metre of floral garlands or per sq ft area covered with flowers?
* If you'd like the florist to make you something outside the look book, provide a picture. Ask them to make you up a sample centrepiece to make sure you're both on the same page about the look. You may need to put this in your agreement—or they may want to charge extra.

Eat Smart: The Caterer

He can define the success of your wedding celebrations more than any other vendor. The best caterers don't advertise—their food speaks for themselves.

When to book

Five months before the wedding, or as soon as you have a date and a venue.

What it costs

Prices vary widely. But to determine price, take into account:

Guests: Number, age group, what proportion with special preferences (veg/non-veg/vegan, Jain, nut- or gluten-free, etc.). What happens if less or more show up? (Always provide for wedding crashers!)

Menu: Which dishes, what level of spices, in what order they should be served, etc.

Serving staff: Number, dress code, any speciality requirements (such as flair bartenders, dosa makers, etc.).

Peripherals: Number and type of water coolers, wash basins, cutlery, crockery, glassware, linen, etc.

Table decorations: Cut fruits and salads, candles, etc.

Place cards: For sit-down dinners.

The caterer interview

* What cuisines do you do?
* Do you have any special menus?
* What extras do you offer, such as live counters or exotic paan and supari stalls?
* Do you provide bar services?
* Do you charge per plate or one fixed amount? What if there are no-shows or excess guests?
* What is your staff strength?
* What is the ratio of waiters to guests?
* Do you provide crockery, cutlery, glassware, table linen, table dressings and portable wash basins?

Great br-ideas

Ask your caterer to do a dry run of the final menu for you and a couple of your friends and relatives a week before the wedding. That way you not only get to see whether the menu and service are the way you want them, but you also get to actually enjoy your own selections, much better than you will on your wedding day.

Also, on your wedding day (if you're not fasting according to your community's tradition), have your caterer bring you and your groom samples of the food before your ceremony and as you're resting between events. You'll want to stay fortified—and not miss any of the hors d'oeuvres and buffet.

Wedding traditions

A Parsi mother of the bride begins the ceremony with a tray filled with raw eggs, supari, rice, coconut, dates and water. She rotates the tray around like an aarti thaali, breaks the eggs on the floor on her right side, smashes the coconut (it must happen in one shot!) and then cracks her knuckles to ward off the evil eye, welcomes the groom and gets on with the wedding rituals.

Pictures Speak a Thousand Words: Photographers and Videographers

The photographer and videographer record all the special moments of your wedding week and give you fabulous albums and beautifully edited videos to share with friends and family for years to come. When choosing your photographer and/or videographer, you should consider:

How many: This depends on how large your guest list is and the various angles you want photographed. For example, some brides are content with the standard options of posed stage photos and family groups, whereas others want simultaneous candids, arty shots, as well as images of the decorations, buffet tables, etc. Videographers, too, can concentrate on the couple, following you around as you meet and greet, or they can go around the party on their own, shooting your husband's nephew doing an impromptu dance or your grandfather regaling a group of youngsters with his war stories. The more types of coverage you want, the more you'll need on the job.

The photographer/videographer interview

* What types of packages do you offer? And in each, how many hours do you shoot at the wedding? How many prints, CDs, DVDs are included, and what is the charge for additional items? How much do you charge to put together albums? How many copies of the wedding DVD will we receive?
* What artistic innovations do you include in your albums/videos?
* How many assistants will you require to photograph my wedding with ___ (number) invitees?
* Will you let me keep a copy of the photo negatives and/or digital photo files or raw video footage?

When to book

You don't need to reserve these chaps more than a month before the big day. And for most professionals, as long as you determine that they're free on the days you need them and confirm with them right before, there's little chance of things going belly up. Most outfits even ensure back-up guys just in case the main men fall ill at the last moment.

What it costs

Costs can vary greatly from Rs 5,000 to 1 lakh (if you want add-ons like on site digital prints to send home with guests, or custom albums for the bride and groom). It's best to fix how many pictures of what sort, how many copies and all the details right at the start.

Must-clicks

* Individual photos of you, him, his mom, his dad, your mom, your dad, both sets of siblings, grandparents, aunts, uncles and best friends. (Have your list of desired posed shots ready!)

* Pics of you and your man with all of the above and some permutations and combinations. Have them click you in front of any interesting scenery your venue offers—greenery and flowers, interesting architecture, etc.

* You and your man with your boss, his boss, and any other special guests.

* Any special moments that you have planned through the function.

* Any spontaneous events you'll want to remember, such as your grandfather overcoming a lifetime of shyness to suddenly sweep your grandma on to the dance floor for the most romantic waltz. A friend or family member may have to be responsible for quickly alerting the videographer to moments like these!

Working with your photographer/videographer

Back-ups: Better safe than sorry, right? In this digital age, there's no harm in nagging your crew to bring enough memory cards, batteries, extension cords, lights, etc..

Event flow: Give your crew a programme so they know exactly where everyone of importance will be and when. Here, too, it's good to have a family member overseeing things. Tip: You may also want to introduce the photographers to immediate family on both sides.

Dress rehearsal: It does help if you just take the photographers through the paces. Decide on the best angles and lighting beforehand.

Choices: Decide on how many posed stills and candids you want (the less formal the wedding function, the more of the latter you'll want) and with what special effects.

Shot list: Give the photographers a list of each permutation of family members for group shots. You don't want to later realise you never took a shot with your favourite cousins. And be sure to have them click a frame-able ensemble picture that includes the bride and groom, both sets of parents and all your siblings.

Click nix: Five things you DON'T want in your party pics

*Red eye, double chin, over—or under—exposed pictures.

* Frozen smiles (this may mean your photo guy took too long to click).

* Drunk uncles and friends in various states of insobriety (though some of the latter can be fun for post-wedding photo parties!).

* Guests jostling at the buffet or stuffing their faces (especially with gulab jamuns).

* Overcandid pictures of dancing couples' sweat-stained attire.

Man with a Plan: Wedding Planner

A wedding planner is a professional event organiser who takes on a specific part of your planning, or your whole multi-day event. Look for a planner who's handled numerous weddings, so that s/he has a wide variety of contacts and can prepare for the unexpected. The tougher part—finding someone you mesh well with. They'll be your trusted rep with vendors, and even family members.

When to book

Start hunting for your wedding planner as soon as you decide you want help planning. Why not start stress-free and in professional hands, right? (See p 28 for tips on picking your wedding planning style.)

What it costs

Wedding planners usually charge a flat fee (from Rs 50,000 to a few lakh) for an event, or for high-priced, intensive jobs, they a charge percentage of the total cost (in the range of 10%). Either way, expect to pay a deposit upfront.

The wedding planner interview

* Would you be able to handle all of the events I'm hosting and need help planning, which include ____(mehendi, engagement, cocktail, reception, etc.)?
* Would you personally attend all of my events? Can you explain how you handle event staffing and supervision?
* What is included in the planning services you offer brides?
* If I hire you, walk me through what happens between now and my wedding. What schedule and systems will you use?
* How do you work with additional vendors? Do you have a list of vendors you prefer to work with?
* Can I use a vendor that you aren't familiar with if I choose?

Working with your wedding planner

Wedding planners can help you with everything from choosing a caterer with the most scrumptious buffet options, to recommending a much-needed spa service to get your skin glowing, to day-of-the-event tasks like making sure your mehendi artist or the bartender arrives on time and that your wait staff opens the buffet at just the right moment. But don't expect a wedding planner to make all the decisions. S/He will give you options, and then talk you through the pros and cons of each so you can take an informed decision.

Have your wedding planner help you:

- Set up realistic figures under each category of your budget.
- Consider wedding size, number of guests, and theme (if applicable)—and give you advice on trends, possibilities and drawbacks of any iffy choices you might be about to make.
- Find all vendors for your venue, catering, music, photography, decorator/florist, stationery, mehendi, etc. Some planners prefer to work with a group of vendors they've pre-approved, so they know ahead of time that the product will be high quality, that the vendor is easy to work with, and that they may be able to help you get a good price.
- Don't hesitate to ask for advice or help with smaller vendors or any other detail—from bridal make-up and hairstylists, to how to present your gifts to the groom and his family, and maybe some help in identifying gift items, too.
- Negotiate contracts with other vendors so you get the most value for money.
- Manage all vendors during the preparation stage and on the day of the event.
- Mediate with family and friends throughout the planning process.
- Prepare your thank you notes, get them signed by you, and post them.
- Our tip: stay involved. Even if the planner is liaising on your behalf, stay in the loop on all approvals and details for final deliveries so you know immediately if things go off course. Have weekly updates early on, and daily updates one or two weeks before wedding week.

Ask the experts

Wedding consultant Neeta Raheja has planned traditional and unique weddings all over India, Canada and the US since the 1990s. She handles mostly big budget affairs, so if a wedding budget doesn't fit her usual range, she'll recommend another planner and then provide support where needed. Her client list includes big names—the Ansals, Mittals, Singhanias and Munjals.

Who is an ideal wedding planner?

Somebody who sits with the bride and her family, and patiently hears their ideas and needs before making suggestions. My USP is 'personalised' service. At every wedding I take on the role of the 'grandmother', guiding and helping, explaining customs, helping them make their celebrations unique.

How can a wedding planner help a bride handle budgeting?

I recommend six months for stress-free planning. I say don't cut corners in an obvious way. The wedding planner should take all the headaches away. The budget's big chunks go away in catering which is dependent on cuisine. You can cut down on the number of guests and ceremonies to save. If you want to do it elegantly, without making people feel as though things have been compromised, do two ceremonies instead of five, but do them well.

How do you keep track of all the details that go into a wedding?

The trick is in knowing the limitations of vendors and constantly checking and rechecking with them about everything. And we are constantly interacting with the bride and her family, helping out with the smallest detail.

Pen Pals: Stationery Designers and Printers

Your wedding stationery is the first chance you get to set the tone of your events for your guests.

Stationery designers create the wedding card, the equivalent to a couture outfit in the world of wedding invites. Since most stationery designers make more than just wedding stationery, you might find your designer by looking out for imaginative visiting cards, personal stationery or invites for other events,

Stationery printers offer readymade options that you can customise. Some will even give you variations on colour, paper size, and texture. It's a bit easier picking a printer, since you can look at their templates and know if one of them is what you're looking for.

Brides who want to be spoiled for choice (from Delhi or elsewhere) head over to Delhi's Chawri Bazaar, which has a whole lane of wedding stationery printers.

The stationery designer or printer interview

* Can I look through samples of your work? Can you show me different grades of paper stock ?

* For printers: Can you personalise your template for me?

* For designers: How do you work? How many options will you show?

* Can you offer embellishment like golden tassels, a supari, or gold dust in a see-through bag?

* How long after approval will it take to print the cards? What happens if there is a discrepancy between the sample I approve and the final lot?

* And how much would it cost if I need additional cards? Do you offer any discount if I print multiple orders with you (programmes, thank you notes, etc.)?

When to book

Send out your invitations four–six weeks before your event so that guests from Calicut to California have ample notice. If you're going to do 'save the date' cards (they can mail up to six months before the wedding), then you can give it a little less time. Either way, you'll need to work backwards to make sure you're approving your proof with enough lead time for printing, addressing, and posting.

What it costs

A wedding card costs approximately Rs 75 (including the envelope and one or two inserts). Prices will vary with paper weight, printing techniques, embellishments, and number of separate cards. The greater your number of invites, the more you'll be able to negotiate on price. Designers will be harder to bargain down. (How much could you negotiate on a Ritu Kumar lehenga, right?) Most designers and printers request a deposit (a negotiable 10–50% of the bill), a second installment when you approve the proof, and the balance when the job is done. Smaller printers may ask for more in advance, might not take the last installment by cheque and usually won't provide a contract.

Working with your stationery designer or printer

With your timeline in mind, you have many decisions before you:

Paper: The thickness, weight, and look: there are tie-and-dye papers, some with flower petals, others embroidered or with a mottled effect, and even paper that looks like leather.

Shape and size: There are the traditional rectangular and square shapes, or you could have leaflets that are round, star shaped or in any other shape. And if you have multiple cards, you could keep them loose, use flaps to hold them in place, or bind them into a booklet. Another fun option: ditch the envelope, fold a circular paper over square cards and seal it with a customised sticker.

Finished look and printing options: Laser-cut printing and embossing work are the best bet for heavier papers. You'll also have to pick a font style and size, as well as ink colour.

Ask to see an example of the type of printing you've selected on your paper to make sure that what seems like a good idea translates just as well.

Possible add-on: Draw a map on the reverse of the invite if your venue is a way-out location. Or include a sketch of the bride's and groom's family trees and a box of sweets, like Bollywood's first family, the Bachchans, did for Abhishek and Ash's wedding announcement. Or if you have a celebrated poet or artist in the family, add words or a miniaturised painting (like M.F. Hussain's younger daughter did).

Packaging: Wrap your card with a gift in a customised carry bag, a box or any other container to suit your style and budget. Or roll up your wedding card like a scroll, hold it in place with a band, and place it in a cushion pouch and then in an envelope.

What information to include in your invite: The names of the bride and the groom, the parents of the bride and parents of the groom, the date and time of event, the name and address of the venue, and who's hosting plus their contact info. You may also want to include directions, your wedding website (if you have one), the dress code or theme (if applicable), or any information.

How many invites and envelopes: A little more than your guest list for any last-minute additions. Get extra envelopes, there's bound to be mistakes while writing addresses.

How to address your envelopes

* Address envelopes by hand in calligraphy. For a modern look, you could incorporate coloured or glitter pens, or type address labels.

* Slip your envelope into an outer envelope with the recipients' full names, titles, and address. Make the inner envelope informal, with just the names. Add any members from the household who are also invited. You can even just use first names.

* Ask your courier to be considerate and make sure they won't staple the cards. You could use a third clear plastic outer envelope. And if you're posting your card (especially overseas), buy fancy stamps .

Ask the experts

Karn Malhotra, owner of Bangalore's Exit Design, answered our wedding card questions:

What are your top tips for a bride to best utilise the service/product a stationery designer has to offer?

* Figure out a few options of cards you like/don't like before meeting vendors—it simplifies the process and reduces chances of time wastage. Define for yourself what is 'experimental' and 'something new'.
* While asking for opinions from family members, ideally, keep that process to a minimum by involving only a few key people—and trust the designer's opinion once you've made the decision to go with him/her.
* Delegate responsibilities once the design is frozen on—you've got other things to attend to!

How can a bride ensure that she varies the cards for her different events while not going over her budget?

Simple variations in colour or textures of paper/fabric are a good option at the design stage. Die cuts, use of accessories, and different printing methods at the production stage. It makes a tremendous difference if a client is clear in her mind about how much she wants to spend overall—which helps us plan better, too.

Is it advisable to hire the same vendor for all the events or separate ones?

It's much simpler to have a single point of contact when it comes to your wedding cards and wedding communication that goes out. Interacting with different vendors—namely, one or two designers, one printer, one fabricator and so on—only complicates matters. It's always advisable to go with one design agency that will take care of the entire process, as much as you might be involved every step of the way.

Class Act: Choreographer

Choreographers offer two main services for weddings. They teach you and your family and friends, routines for the sangeet or mehendi, or a rehearsed 'first dance' for the bride and groom. Sometimes they also organise performances at these events. To find a choreographer, check out the better-known dance studios or professional dance companies in your city, as they usually offer wedding choreography.

Here are some details you'll need to share with the choreographer—have them ready before you meet.

What you have in mind for the entertainment: Is it a series of short dances to a hit song that you and your family will perform, and which will have to be taught to you? Is it a skit about your personal fairy tale of how you and your honey ended up with each other? If so, do you need the choreographer to write the script or will you do it yourself (maybe with the help of

The choreographer interview

* Are you free on the dates we'll need you? Will you be free to perform on my wedding dates? Or, can you schedule training sessions for our family beforehand?
* Who will train us? (Will you teach us yourself, or send your team?)
* What will the schedule of lessons be like? What type of commitment are the dancers required to make?
* Can you show me videos of past performances you choreographed?
* What theme ideas can you offer?
* Where will the training sessions happen? Do you have studio space convenient for everyone involved? (Most often, rehearsals happen at the bride's house because everyone knows where it is and it's often the most convenient location for out-of town guests. If your place isn't big enough or is filled with a zillion relatives, do ask this question).

your sister-in-law who's a writer, or suggestions from family and friends brainstorming over your mom's famous aloo parathas)?

How long do you want the performances, and for how many events? How many people will be dancing (beware of drop-outs!). Most choreographers charge for their teaching time by the hour, and will need to estimate how many teaching hours you'll need.

Or, do you simply want the dance troupe to perform a special routine and then encourage all the guests to jump onto the dance floor for an evening of free-form dancing?

When to book

You should ideally book your choreographer two months before the wedding. The busier artists will often request that you book them four months in advance. The latest you should approach this vendor should be one month before—you have to give your dancers (who might include older aunties and distracted younger cousins) a little training time, or the professional troupe a little lead time to choreograph exactly the right routine for your wedding.

What it costs

Choreographer rates depend on how well known the studio or dancer is, the number of people dancing in your group and the number of teaching hours needed. Arati Sunawala from Tarantismo in Bangalore charges Rs 700–1,000 per hour, depending on the size of the group dancing. She recommends 2–5 lessons per dance, and that you plan to have multiple smaller groups dancing, with maybe one larger grand finale. Lourd Vijay, who runs another dance company in Bangalore, charges Rs 7,500 for 5 sessions. In Delhi, top choreographers like Rajesh Khalwa or Divya Miglani charge between Rs 50,000 and Rs 1.5 lakh, and others like Mansi Aggarwal are more reasonable at about Rs 25,000 for a 45-minute performance. The Terence Lewis Contemporary Dance Company (TLCDC) in Mumbai, with its many years of experience and shows all over the world, charges about Rs 50,000 for two instructors to teach a group a three-minute song over a week. You may have to also budget in recording studio charges if you're mixing together music and dialogues for a skit. These charges are usually in the range of Rs 300–1,000 per hour of production time.

Most dance companies charge a flat rate if they're providing the dancers. To perform a dance or a skit, Tarantismo charges around Rs 50,000. Terence Lewis's company charges anywhere between Rs 5 and 10 lakh depending on the duration of the act, how new the piece is, and whether the lead dancer, Terence Lewis, has been asked to perform.

Some choreographers may ask for the whole payment upfront at the first session, and others will take an advance amount and the remainder at the last session. Lourd Vijay has his clients sign a registration form and disclaimer that includes rules about cancellations and rescheduling policies.

Ask the experts

Arati Sunawala from Tarantismo in Bangalore gives some tips on how to make the most of your choreography sessions.

Because you're usually paying per hour, schedule rehearsals cleverly. Let people know this schedule in advance so everyone can come, preferably in the evenings after the work or school day. Make the dance get-togethers a fun event—not like a mandatory class. Have snacks and drinks for everyone—it can be a great way to bond with your family and friends.

Music to Your Ears: The DJ

A disc jockey (or DJ) plays a mix of music for pre-wedding parties like sangeets, mehendis or cocktails, as well as for the wedding and reception.

Some brides prefer to handle the music themselves—and that works for smaller, more informal parties where you can just burn a bunch of CDs or load up your iPod with your fave tunes. For the larger parties, do go ahead and hire a professional—it'll be worth it so you (or your brother) can relax.

According to Raghu Subramaniam from Phase One Events, Bangalore, a bride should get a fix on the type of crowd that will be at her party, and hire a DJ who has expertise in the genres of music her guests will like. It's best to use the same DJ for all your wedding functions. Sometimes though, the same DJ can do a variety of genres if you want different genres for different events—Bollywood or Tollywood hits for the sangeet and mehendi, lounge or house music for the reception. Do check if the DJ you're interested in can play all of these. Our tip on where to find a great DJ: check with the nightclubs in your city.

Most importantly, avoid snooty DJs who will impose their taste on your guests. Chat with the DJ to suss out his personality ahead of time.

The DJ interview

* What type(s) of music do you play?
* Do you provide sound and lighting equipment and what do you recommend for my venue and numbers?
* Do you prefer to play a fixed set, or will you take requests?

When to book

Start looking out for this all-important person two months before the wedding.

What it costs

The average cost for a young, non-celeb DJ in India is about Rs 25,000 per night (this includes sound and lighting). A more experienced DJ would charge around Rs 35,000, and a newer DJ might cost only around Rs 10,000 (also young could mean innovative). If you want an original sound, though, be prepared to shell out. India's top party DJs like DJ Suketu, DJ Nasha or DJ Aqueel will charge anywhere from Rs 2 to Rs 6 lakh per night (you might be able to negotiate and get them to throw in an extra party). You'll get fabulous mixes and an experienced DJ who can gauge the crowd and play exactly what they want, varying the mood through the evening.

When fixing their price, DJs take into account how long they'll have to play, the size of the crowd, and the wattage needed for equipment. Often not included in their price are rentals of sound, mixing equipment (CDs, turntables) and lights, as well as current wedding trends like laser lighting. Some DJs will require an advance (usually 50%) and the rest about a week after the event. Others may ask for payment upfront.

Wedding traditions

The sister of the bride, especially if she's younger, often gets teased by the groom as saali adhi gharwali (implying his lien over her as the bride's sister). This tradition originates from the days when if a woman died early or in childbirth, her husband often married her younger sister.

Working with your DJ

Talk to your DJ about the kind of mood you want to create. DJ Jasmeet from Bangalore suggests, 'It's always better if the bride informs the vendor what she truly has in mind for the wedding. I advise most of my clients to mail me a list of their favourite tracks prior to the wedding.' (Our tip: Tell your DJ which songs you DON'T want played as well.) Figure out whether you want a retro party, disco bash, a Bollywood masala eve or a salsa soirée, tell the DJ, and then trust him to put it together for you. Or to be even more thorough, you can schedule a meeting with him about 2 weeks prior to the event and go through the tunes he has chosen.

Top Bollywood shaadi tracks from DJ Clement in Mumbai

'Chaiya chaiya', Dil Se
'Chunari chunari', Monsoon Wedding
'Mujhse shaadi karogi', Mujhse Shadi Karogi
'Jawani janeman', Namak Halal
'Yeh mera dil', Don
'Saat samundar', Vishwatma
'Mehendi laga ke rakhna', Dilwale Dulhaniya Le Jayenge
'Dus bahane', Dus
'Right here right now', Bluffmaster

Also, make sure you're both comfortable with his POA: keeping to a predetermined set and/or taking requests. And get your DJ's assistance or advice on how to hire good equipment.

Your Right Hand: Mehendi Artist

Don't go crazy interviewing every mehendi artist in town. There are several artists in every city, and the good ones' reputations usually precede them. If you're attending a wedding a few months before your own, do check to see if you like the mehendi artists. Most bring albums with pictures of their past work to help brides and their guests choose what they want, as well as to advertise their work. Grab their visiting card if you like the work.

Or go with one reco from a trusted source, check the cost and book the artist—ask questions about styles, designs, etc. closer to the wedding.

If you're looking for a non-traditional application or a particular design, ask about new trends or different styles. If you want a famous, nationally known artist, check out bridal magazines and the net for ideas (even lesser-known artists now can be found in these, as many of them are savvy professionals). You can take note of which artists work for celebrity weddings, if you're willing to spend for the privilege of getting your mehendi done by the same hands that did Aishwarya's.

Neha, a Delhi bride, flew in a mehendiwali from Gujarat, as this community is known for applying henna well. But keep in mind that if you import a mehendi artist, you'll have to pay for flights, transport, lodging, food, in addition to the actual expenses of the mehendi night. Mehendi artists often speak Hindi or the local language, so if you're not familiar with either, take a translator along. An ideal task for your wedding planner if you have one—though Sheila aunty will do just as well!

When to book

You need to book a mehendi artist a few months before your wedding because the superior artists get booked up far in advance. 'You should contact us at the same time you're booking your wedding venue,' says Seema Divecha, one of Bangalore's most sought-after mehendiwalis.

What it costs

The cost of mehendi depends on the reputation of the artist, the amount of detail involved, and the surface area being adorned. According to mehendi artist, Seema Divecha, average costs for a big city would be:

Bridal mehendi: Anywhere between Rs 1,500 for a simple design for the hands, to Rs 10,000 for an application up to the elbows and knees.

For other guests: Rs 50–75 for the palm, Rs 100–150 for a full hand (front and back). Having a beauty parlour apply your mehendi might be as much as double these figures in cities like Delhi and Mumbai.

Your artist may ask for an advance payment of 10–20% to confirm the booking, although it's rare that they ask for a deposit at all.

Mehendi tips

- Mehendi variations: mehendi tattoos, zardozi work mehendi, using two types of mehendi such as maroon with black outline, nail polish mehendi and glitter non-permanent paint. For a trendier look, get the artists to do henna tattoos on upper arms, ankles, midriff or back. You can experiment with colour as well. Black mehendi looks stunning, which is why many like it, but it has the potential to cause allergies on sensitive skin because besides henna, it also contains phenylenediamine, or PPD, a chemical which gives it its jet-black colour—so be sure to do a patch test before you use it
- Call the mehendi artists early (even before the formal start of your mehendi party) because a bridal application can take from 2–13 hours, depending on how intricate or full you want it, and how high you want to go on your hands and feet. You'll want time to dance

and mingle when you're not sitting still, and have time left over for your friends and family to get their mehendi put on without having too long a wait.

- If your mehendi is intricate or you have a large group, ask the artist to bring lots of assistants. Perhaps ask her to allocate the more experienced assistants to the more demanding guests; the ones with the less laborious and traditional designs for the younger or less fussy ones.
- Here's a fun idea: get the mehendiwali to write your groom's initials somewhere in the intricate design on your hand. Then on your wedding night, have the groom try to find it. If he doesn't, you'll be in charge for life!
- Ensure a deeper colour for your mehendi by keeping it on for at least two hours after it is applied. Adding sesame or eucalyptus oil to the paste before it's applied makes the red deepen to a rich burgundy. When it's dry, dab on a lemon juice and sugar mixture that the mehendi artists will know about and put on for you if your friends don't have their hands free. Then scrape it off. DO NOT WET. Dip a ear bud in olive or avocado oil and remove the bits of the henna that don't come off with the scraping. If you want even more colour, depending on body heat, warm your hands and feet over a tava for a while. (The darker your mehendi, say the old wives, the more your mother-in-law—or sometimes husband—will love you!)
- Wash only after 12 hours, as water and soap hinder the darkening process. If you must bathe, avoid the areas where mehendi has been applied. Some mehendi artists suggest wrapping your hands and feet in plastic shower caps before your bath, and getting someone to help you wash.
- In case you do stain your lovely Anamika Khanna ghagra, wait till the mehendi dries and then scrape it off. Don't panic and try to wash it off.
- Aftercare: Avoid chlorinated water and saunas as they cause mehendi to fade faster.

Pretty as a Package: Party Favours Vendor

It's tradition (and just plain old fun) for the hosts of bridal showers, mehendi parties and sometimes hen parties to send guests home with a little parting gift. Most brides don't go to different vendors for their favours but double up with another vendor.

When to book

Make sure you give the vendor enough time before the wedding to source, customise, show you samples for approval, and to go into production. This is usually a period of 14–20 days before the party.

What it costs

Prices vary and are negotiable depending on the extent of additional services the vendor is providing for your wedding (décor, wedding planning, mehendi, etc.). Include the favours in any written agreement.

The favours vendor interview

* What kinds of favours can you source or produce for me? Will they be unique or do you do similar things for all weddings?
* Are we on the same page as far as style and colours are concerned?
* Will you be able to deliver the favours well in time?
* What are the latest trends in party favours that you'd recommend for my party?
* How much in advance do I need to place the order with you?
* How much will the favours cost to source or customise, and then get packaged? (As far as possible, you will need to describe the size of the favour, the numbers you need, the packaging you want, and the occasion it's for so the vendor can give you an accurate price quote.)

Choosing a favours vendor

If you're using a wedding planner, they can help you get customised favours made or sourced. It's important for you to check the finish of the product so do look at their samples from other weddings. Here are some ideas for vendors and sourcing gifts:

- Several florists and decorators supply favours and offer gift wrapping. Vendors who make chocolates can supply them in customised shapes for your parties.
- Most mehendi artists can bring the mehendi party favours—they might even offer you a better deal on the mehendi if they can also handle the gifts.
- For readymade favours, try the local markets. In Bangalore, the Gujjri Bazaar, opposite Russel Market, is a treasure trove of unusual items, as is Crawford Market in Mumbai, or Karol Bagh, Palika Bazaar and Dilli Haat in Delhi. Small markets like Hanuman Mandir in Delhi and Ulsoor Market in Bangalore sell reasonably priced bindis and bangles in a staggering variety.
- If you have contacts within your local theatre or film circles, check with them for unusual costumes or exotic props like handcuffs or tiaras.
- Archies is great for favours as well like photo frames, stuffed toys and CDs.

Working with your party favours vendor

A good vendor will customise gifts for you to match the colours of your mehendi or the theme of your hen night, or even the design on your wedding card or lehenga. For mehendis, common favours are bangles and bindis in cane baskets, and pouches with dry fruit and vermilion powder, paan and mehendi cones. Kalpana Rajaram from Petal Talks in Bangalore organises favours like candles, chocolates and sweets, or specialities relevant to a particular culture. For one mehendi for a Goan boy and a Maharashtrian girl, Rajaram included a sarong and cashew feni and had a big straw hat tied around the gift basket. For hen parties and bridal showers, just beginning to be popular in India, fun favours like chocolates in naughty shapes or filled with liquor or champagne are the norm.

(See our section on pre-wedding parties on pp 115-62 for more ideas.)

Sailing Away

The Honeymoon

You've had your big day, so now it's time to get away. The honeymoon can be even more fun than getting married. It's the most stress-free time you're going to share, before things like family, careers, kids and other responsibilities kick in. Whether it's a three-day uber-exclusive getaway or a month of backpacking, you need to spend some time planning your honeymoon. Of course, a word of warning—any travel plans are subject to external factors. So be flexible and know that even if things don't go exactly the way you planned them, you'll still have fun together and strengthen your relationship.

No one knows the exact origins of this sweet-sounding word, but it is said that the idea of couples taking a holiday together after their wedding first became popular in the late 1800s. One speculation is that new love's ardour wanes even as it waxes to the fullest, just like the moon, and hence the month after the wedding is the month when love's in full bloom and 'as sweet as honey'. Another possible origin of the word is from the Babylonian practise whereby the groom was supposed to be given as much 'mead' as he wanted (for happiness and fertility) by the bride's family for an entire month after the wedding. As mead is made from honey, it made sense to call this month a 'honeymoon'.

Ask the experts: Top honeymoon spots

Manoj Nair, manager, corporate communications, for the Travel Corporation of India, shared the most popular picks for honeymoon destinations:

International

Australia and New Zealand
Italy (either alone or as a stop on a Mediterranean cruise)
Maldives
Mauritius
Switzerland

Domestic

Goa is the perennial favourite
Kerala (holiday in a houseboat on the backwaters and Munnar)
Lakshadweep or Andaman Islands
Ooty, Kodaikanal, Coorg
Shimla, Manali, Nainital

Ready reckoner: What kind of destination should you choose?

- Home stays

It's like staying at your relative's house, with all the cleanliness and wholesome meals, but without the fuss and bother. And, enough privacy to make those special memories.
Best for: couples who want a quiet holiday surrounded by nature, and are game to try home comforts over five-star standards—or just prefer them over the sometimes impersonal five-star experience.

- Resorts

These are zones dedicated to holidaying, everything specially created for your leisure and pleasure. From accommodation to meals, to entertainment and workouts, to activities and sightseeing, everything is centred around your needs. Beach, forest, lake or hill resorts or even mountain chalets and log huts are all super options.
Best for: couples who love large buffets and fun activities, especially if they're organised and bacteria-free.

- Cruises

Like resorts, but on water. From Norwegian fjords to the Mediterranean seas, from luxury liners on the Nile to refurbished houseboats on the Kerala backwaters—cruises allow you the luxury of going from place to place without having to pack and repack your bags. You can spend quality time with each other, have a ball of a time with onboard dining, entertainment and activities, and see some fabulous places each time the ship drops anchor. Another plus of this experience is that once you've embarked, you don't deal with cash at all. Most meals and entertainment are included in the per-person rate, and you can charge extras to your cabin card, so you can truly have a hands-free (no money clip, no cellphone) and hassle free honeymoon.
Best for: couples who find being on the water romantic and want to see the world but don't want to deal with early morning short-stop flights and unreliable hotel rooms.

* Backpacking trips

  If your wedding budget didn't quite extend to the honeymoon, never mind. A backpacking trip through interesting new places is just as likely to make sparks fly between the two of you as anything else. Of course, you may not quite enjoy the privacy of a room at The Dorchester in the youth hostel dormitory.

  Best for: couples on a budget or the really adventurous, hardy type who turn up their noses at package tours and luxe hotels.

* Drive throughs

  A new trend is to get package holidays that include a week's trailer vacation in New Zealand or a luxury vehicle that you can drive yourself through Europe. This way, you get a feel of the countryside and get to stay in authentic and quaint local inns. Also, you have control over where you're going and what you're doing when, while covering a lot of ground.

  Best for: couples who like the freedom and flexibility to go where they like and stop according to their own schedule.

Wedding traditions

When a bride in the Sindhi community arrives home after her wedding, the groom's parents rinse her feet at the threshold of her new home. Then the bride and groom begin the datar ritual; the new bride enters the house and sprinkles milk in all corners of the house. She places a handful of salt in her husband's hand, which he passes back into her hands, careful not to spill any of it. The ritual is performed three times.

MORRIS

Cruise classics: Our *Wedding Belles* recommendations

7-day Mediterranean cruise on the *Costa Serena*

Plush cabins with private balconies facing the azure Mediterranean. A fabulous spa experience at the on-board Samsaara Spa for you, an exciting F1 simulator for him, scores of fantastic shore excursions, Michelin star cuisine, swimming pools, nightclub, casino as well as a full-scale theatre to keep both of you absolutely entertained.

Cost: Starts from Rs 1 lakh for both of you (exclusive of airfare to and fro embarkation and disembarkation ports).
Best season: April to October

3-day South China sea cruise on the *Super Star Aquarius* or *Super Star Virgo*

The friendliest staff, lavish buffet spreads, wine tastings, yoga classes, super entertainment, and a chance to visit Hong Kong, Xiamen, Singapore and a host of other ports.

Cost: Starts at approximately Rs 50,000 for a 5 night cruise for two people in an inside stateroom on deck 5 and goes up to approximately Rs 2,45,000 for two people in an executive suite on deck 9 or 10 (exclusive of airfare to and fro embarkation and disembarkation ports).
Best season: April to October

5-day Kerala backwaters cruise on the *Oberoi MV Vrinda*

Three nights in the super-luxe cabins on board the superbly fitted-out, double-hull *Motor Vehicle Vrinda* that cruises the backwaters of Lake Vembanad. Gourmet cuisine and very well-organised shore excursions. One night in a deluxe suite at the Trident Kochi.

Cost: Approximately Rs 70,000 for both of you (exclusive of airfare to and from Kochi).
Best season: November to April

Real-life Wedding Belles:

Joeanna and Sandeep, 29 December, 2007, Goa

Joeanna, a journalist, and Sandeep, a PR account manager, went on their honeymoon to Singapore. Joeanna spoke to us about her memorable trip.

What did you pack? How important is it to get all your clothes and accessories just right?
Honestly, I packed more for a holiday than a honeymoon. I did throw in bits of lingerie, but apart from these, the usual dresses, shorts, tops and a swimsuit. It was the weather I was kitting up for, and not my husband! I saw honeymoon pictures of a friend who followed the honeymoon formula and I realised she had a different outfit for every evening! She told me she'd gone shopping to Mango and other high-end stores and her honeymoon pics looked like a fashion spread (also like the Kingfisher calendar—yes, she had multiple swimsuits!). I, on the other hand, traipsed down Colaba Causeway for summer dresses. I made no effort to accessorise and looked quite raggedy in the pics.

Did you have any 'adjustment issues' with your hubby?
Few, really. I've known him since he was this high [points to waist], and am familiar with most of his eccentricities and bad manners!

Was it very difficult to share space with him for the first time?
He took up most of the bed and all of the quilt and that got irritating. But it was nothing I couldn't negotiate!

Were there any issues that came up in the honeymoon that you weren't aware of (him snoring, you taking too long in the shower, etc.)? If yes, how did you deal with them?
Too long in the shower—but that was him, not me. Fist-pounding on the door and threats did the trick.

Bag chat: What to pack for your honeymoon

Essentials

Travel light. Account for one outfit per day, with at least one fresh tee or top for that respective day. Carry jeans, shorts or capris that can be reused. Pack a couple of extras, just in case you have an 'I-hate-everything-I've-brought day' or get drenched or dirty. Check if you're going to have formal dinners, which you will if you're on a cruise. If yes, pack a dress. Accessorise to add variety. If you're balking at the idea of repeating clothes, remember your hubby will probably notice the heavy bag he's carting up the stairs, or the excess baggage fines, more than your wearing the same stunning dress three nights in a row. We're pretty sure you don't need to be told that delicate lingerie and sleepwear are honeymoon staples. Depending on where you're going, also pack speciality garments like swimwear, warm clothes, umbrellas, trekking shoes, riding gear, safari outfits, etc.

Gadgets

You obviously don't want to spend long plane journeys on your honeymoon solo, plugged into your iPod, but perhaps an MP3 player with speakers for your hotel room to set that mood music could be fun. And bring along a travel pack of a favourite board game or a pack of cards. A digi or handycam is de rigueur these days, but don't forget your battery chargers, extra batteries, extra memory cards and USB cables for transferring pictures. Leave the BlackBerry (definitely) and mobile phones (try!) home, or leave them off, unless you're in a lonely or risky place where you need a phone in case of an emergency.

Love stack

Here's where you open the naughty stuff your friends gifted you at the hen bash. Bring aromatic massage oil, chocolate body paint, feathers—your imagination's the limit.

Positive attitude

Probably the single most useful thing you'll take, next to mosquito repellent. If you miss out on the Temple of Luxor because your Nile cruise got stuck at the Esna lock, don't spend the rest of your Egyptian honeymoon blaming each other. As newly-wed Shikha recommends, 'Focus more on spending quality time with each other than on being tourists.'

Sharath
Nithya

Ask the experts: Adventurous honeymoons

Aloke Bajpai, CEO of The Explorers, an outfit that organises exciting outdoorsy trips, has often helped out just-marrieds with an off-the-beaten-track itinerary. He says, 'The best way for a couple to bond is to go off on a trek together.' Here are his recommendations.

High altitude

The Nubra valley region in northern Ladakh is stunning. You get there through the Khardungla Pass (world's highest motorable road). There are some good hotels and you can go for long walks, visit the monasteries, or take a ride on a double-humped camel.

Hill stations

Kinnaur in Himachal Pradesh, almost bordering Tibet, has a small town called Kalpa and a little hamlet called Chitkul. There are no hotels, only some beautiful and well-equipped camps and scenic beauty all around. Pitthoragarh in Uttaranchal, the starting point for the Kailash Manasarovar pilgrimage trek, is fantastic. There are also some undeniably beautiful places like Garhwal, Kausani, Chaukori and Binsar. A village called Lachung in northern Sikkim's Yum Phang valley is simply divine too. Else, there's always Munnar, or Madikeri in Coorg.

Beaches

Lakshadweep, though breathtakingly beautiful, has its limitations as getting permits is difficult. You could visit the privately run Bangaram Island if you crave luxury.

Forests

Wyanad in northern Kerala has plenty of wildlife and natural beauty. There are some lovely treetop lodges to stay in as well.

Historic

Hampi–Badami–Pattadakal or Konarak–Puri and most historic places in India add romance to your honeymoon.

Budget

Pachmarhi in Madhya Pradesh is accessible, cheap and serene.

Outbound

Bhutan is a beautiful destination that Indians are only just discovering.

Happily Ever After

Your Post-Wedding Life Together

So the deed's done. The knot's tied, the mehendi is fading and you've recovered your sleep and your sanity after a sunny, two-week honeymoon in Goa. You're excited about starting your new life together. You're also exploring new dynamics in your relationship with your husband and getting to know his family and friends (if you don't already, but even then, you're getting to know them as Mr and Mrs). Plus, there are all those new expectations of wifely behaviour you're managing—from you, your husband, his family and yours

Your first year of marriage will be bursting with joy, surprises and, hopefully, not too many stumbling blocks. It's best to go in prepared.

But before you leap into the nitty-gritty of settling in, make sure you've dotted your i's, crossed your t's and closed the book on your wedding celebrations. Protocol (and enthusiastic friends and family) demand certain post-wedding bits and bobs. To help you out, we've put together another to-do list below (yup, just when you'd thought your life would be to-do list-free.) We recommend ticking off these items as soon as you can, while you're still in action mode, riding high on the wedding and honeymoon energy—or you'll risk procrastinating and not getting them done until your first anniversary.

Wedding traditions

In a traditional wedding in the Tamil Shaivite community, the bride's brother shows his support for his sister's marriage by offering her a handful of puffed rice grains. The bride hands the puffed rice to the bridegroom, who feeds it to the fire on her behalf during the laaja homam ceremony. This ceremony has special significance; the bride's brother, with this gesture, helps to join the two families in a bond that will last as long as the couple is married.

The Wedding Belles Post-wedding To-do List

Thank you notes

Every guest made the effort to come and be with you for your big day—and they gave you fantastic gifts, which are making your new home look like a model house straight out of *Elle Décor*. Your second cousins from Nellore and family friends from Gulmarg travelled in for the festivities. Your sister helped you come up with the pink and orange theme for your mehendi, and your best friends were oh so patient waiting around while you made the difficult choice between a zardozi-or Swarovski-encrusted lehenga. Your brother efficiently coordinated your guests' accommodation and transport. And your parents—where do you even begin to thank them?

Say it from the heart

It's important that you express your gratitude to all of your loved ones and guests personally. A handwritten card is always the most thoughtful and proper way to thank someone for a gift. Though, if you have a huge wedding, it's acceptable to pre-print notes that you give to guests either at the reception or mail to them afterwards. 'If you've had the Big Fat Indian Wedding, hand writing all the notes would be tedious,' etiquette expert Rukshana Eisha says. 'Pre-printed ones make more sense. But you could send handwritten ones to people who made the effort to come from out of town.'

Etiquette dictates that you should send thank you cards within a few months of your wedding. The more personal your sentiments the better, but you don't have to start from scratch for each note. It's alright to send a similar message to people who are roughly in the same category; formal notes to in-laws or personal ones to friends (see p 248 for a template thank you note).

If you do want to mail everyone a thank you note, use your wedding list for reference and work your way down through the names. You can also divide up the work: have your fiancé take care of his personal friends and friends of his family, and ask your parents if they'll help by calling or writing to your family and their friends who attended—this is perfectly fine. One bride we spoke to saved time by hiring someone to handwrite the thank you messages she composed in the cards for her. At the end, she simply signed the cards and sent them out. Do whatever it takes to make it happen!

What types of cards work best? Most big stationery stores and bookshops have blank thank you cards, ranging from the poetic to the humorous. Shweta, who got married in Bangalore and France in late 2007, sourced beautiful Ganeshaa batik cards from Bangalore's big stationer, Gangaram's, and wrote personal messages inside. You can also print custom cards that match your wedding invitations, or just something that strikes your fancy. Nazia, from Bangalore, designed her thank you cards at the same time as her wedding cards, using the same colour and design scheme: handmade paper with a paisley block print, created by a rural women's NGO that she supports. Another idea—attach pre-printed thank you notes to a favour you'll send home with guests at your reception, like a small box of chocolates or mithai in your wedding colours, a small silver coin or diya with your names inscribed on it, or, if you're into the green scene, perhaps a packet of seeds they can grow to help them remember your special day. (For more on designing and printing cards, see pp 216-19).

If you'd rather save trees and time with an e-thank you, go ahead. In today's cyber-friendly world, many brides are choosing to send their thanks via email, especially if they've had guests attend from all over the world. Even though your mother might frown on your sending an email, she and any naysayers would agree that it's far better than no thank you at all. Here's how to do it. You can send out a common email to most of your guests. We suggest mailing it to yourself and bcc'ing your guests—even if this is a tad impersonal, it's far better than throwing up your hands and claiming that your 1,500 or 600 or 350 guests are too many to thank! But if you have the time, you can try to send a separate email addressed to each individual or family, rather than sending out a mass mail. Or send personalised emails to the people you feel were extra generous and/or helpful. Of course, you may have to customise things and take a few steps backwards for your old aunty from Ranchi who hasn't heard of Gmail quite yet—send her a card via postal mail or make that personal phone call. She'll appreciate the effort. You may also want to call or write cards to a select list of the most important people: VIP guests, respected elders, and/or in-laws. For example, after her wedding, Kapila, a food and hospitality consultant from Bangalore, emailed all her guests, except the friends of her in-laws. Kapila sent these guests thank you cards because she felt she needed to be more formal with them, and thank them properly.

Channelling your inner Shakespeare to compose your thank you notes can seem tough—especially if you know you have to write hundreds. In the next page is our recipe for the perfect thank you card. It might be too much work to personalise every letter, so modify this to your taste.

Sample thank you note

Dear [insert name],

Thank them specifically for gift so they know it reached you safely.
Thank you so much for the wonderful blender.

Say how you'll put it to good use.
We both love making smoothies, and can't wait to have you over to taste our strawberry-banana concoction.

Thank them for being at the wedding, and if applicable, for anything they did to help with the wedding, travelling from far away, being such good friends to the family, etc.
We were touched that you came from so far for our wedding and we'll always remember your dance at the sangeet. We're very lucky to have such loving cousins.

Closing.
Much love, Richa and Raj
Or
All our best wishes, Richa and Raj

Changing Your Name

Most brides happily adopt their husband's surname. This age-old tradition is followed all over India as a convention that makes in-laws happy and gives you, your husband and (eventually) your children a sense of belonging and unity in the family name.

Taking her husband's name felt natural for Anjali, who moved to Calicut, Kerala, when she married planter Sanjay. 'No one reacted, as it was the normal thing to do,' she remembers 'I don't think that changing my name has any real impact on my individuality. Plus, with the same surname, it feels more like being part of the same family.'

If you are going to change your name, make sure to change them in all your documents—simultaneously, if possible (see adjacent box). This is also applicable to your change of address.

Identity crisis

* Driver's licence
* Passport
* Every credit card in your wallet
* Bank accounts
* Bank lockers, memberships, subscriptions to societies and clubs
* Income tax and other tax returns
* Ration card (if you're still using one)
* Leases or deeds to any property
* The LPG connection
* Voter's card
* Frequent-flyer cards
* Store or hotel rewards cards
* Email address (or you can just have email forwarded from this email address to your new one)
* Online profiles (Gmail, Linkedin, Facebook, Orkut etc.)

The process

Changing your name in India requires a legal procedure, which includes newspaper publication, filing an affidavit, etc. However, to change your surname after marriage you only need to sign the marriage certificate, and your name is changed. So, be sure to register your wedding to get that certificate. (See pp 170–2 for more on how to register your marriage.)

You'll then need to make a list of documents that have your maiden name on them, especially your current forms of identification—they will need to be changed (see box). Some of these documents and ID changes require lengthy procedures, but most can be easily amended with a formal letter and proof of marriage.

For example, to change your surname for your passport, fill out the application and submit it along with your original passport, a photocopy of your husband's passport and a photocopy of your marriage certificate (see passport.gov.in/cpv/checklist.htm). Note: Remember to do your research well before the wedding—you don't want to be stuck with no passport one day before your honeymoon! At work, if you're known by your maiden name, send out an email to clients or vendors, and an office memo informing everyone of the change in your surname.

The pros and cons

For women who change their last names, there's an added bonus: handling bureaucratic processes like bank accounts, kids' school admissions and visas all become easier when you and your husband share the same last name. 'It is way easier to change your surname in India than to keep your maiden last name,' warns Sasha, a media professional from Mumbai who married in 2006 and opted out of the name change game. 'I have to hear moral lectures from everyone from a club membership clerk to a voter ID worker. Paperwork is a lot tougher when you don't change your name. A LOT. So do it only if you are as attached to it as I am.' Even courier companies have been known to sometimes refuse to let you accept important deliveries in your husband's name, unless you have some sort of ID with the same last name to prove that you're related, says one bride.

Keeping your maiden name is still a fairly bold step in India, unless your families are extremely progressive. But if you're well established in your career under your maiden name, or just attached to it because you feel like it defines you, you can keep your name against the odds, adopt a hyphenated one, or just keep both (if the two names together are not too much of a mouthful). This is especially helpful with things like work references where your maiden name features. One option is to use your maiden name as your middle name, which allows you to use it when you want to, depending on the situation. Or for a truly egalitarian approach, try this: When Monisha Jaising, a TV producer from Bangalore, married Rohit Vaid, also a TV professional, from Mumbai in April 2006, they both took each other's names—they became Monisha Jaising Vaid and Rohit Jaising Vaid—and that's how their names have appeared in their shows' credit rolls ever since.

Another option, if you're torn between convenience and convention, is to follow Kaveri, a bride from Bangalore who married in January 2004. She hasn't changed her name officially, but uses her husband's name when it suits her, socially and professionally. She and her husband work together, so when they are presenting to clients, she uses his last name, so they present a professional, united front, while all her legal documents are still in her maiden name to avoid the formalities of changing it.

Whatever your decision, try to have the name-changing conversation with your fiancé early on—it can be a sensitive issue . Radhika, who grew up and married in Bangalore but now lives in New York, resolved the issue quickly one memorable day. 'We hadn't talked about this changing name thing at all. When we went to register our marriage at City Hall in New York, they asked if I wanted to change my name—I said no. Deepak, who comes from a much more conservative family than mine, looked at me and asked why not. I asked him if he wanted to change his name, he said no. End of story.'

Wedding pictures and videos

We haven't yet met a bride who isn't dying to get her hands on her wedding pictures. The memories are sure to cure any blues when the excitement around D-Day abates (believe us, brides do get the post-wedding blues). Once you get the pictures back, you'll get to spend some time sifting through all the photos, and to pick and choose the film-star shots. Some photographers make an album for you. Most wedding video packages include delivery of an edited video within a couple of months. Usually videographers ask you for your preferences before they put together a final production. You'll have told him who and what to capture on film. (See working with videographers, pp 208-10.) Now, after the wedding, be sure to instruct the video guy about the kind of video editing you want—a compact montage of short vignettes, or footage of every event in detail. You could even give him a CD of your favourite songs to use as the soundtrack!

Sharing the memories

- The easiest way to share wedding photos with your family and friends is to post them to your personal wedding website (make one at ConnectedWeddings.com). Or try a free photo-share website like zoomin.com or snapfish.com—they'll let you print your photos, make cups and calendars, ship them anywhere in India and abroad. Kodakgallery.com, flickr.com (owned by Yahoo and accessible through any Yahoo email ID) and picasa.com (owned by Google and accessible through any Gmail email ID) don't offer prints (either in India or at all), but let you upload and share photos. Just sign up for an account on the site of your choice, upload your digital pictures, and invite your friends to view them online. Alternatively, it's also easy to share photos by posting a digital album to your profile on a social networking site like Orkut or Facebook.
- Alternatively, burn a bunch of the most fun pictures and/or a short video on CDs and distribute to guests. One couple, Kaveri and Anshul, had a friend design a kitschy CD cover with a picture of them hanging onto a gaily coloured auto rickshaw—which was, quirkily, their ride back to their hotel after the wedding.

Wedding pictures and videos

We haven't yet met a bride who isn't dying to get her hands on her wedding pictures. The memories are sure to cure any blues when the excitement around D-Day abates (believe us, brides do get the post-wedding blues). Once you get the pictures back, you'll get to spend some time sifting through all the photos, and to pick and choose the film star shots. Some photographers make an album for you. Most wedding video packages include delivery of an edited video within a couple of months. Usually videographers ask you for your preferences before they put together a final production. You'll have told him who and what to capture on film. (See working with videographers, pp 208-10.) Now, after the wedding, be sure to instruct the video guy about the kind of video editing you want—a compact montage of short vignettes, or footage of every event in detail.You could even give him/her a CD of your favourite songs to use as the soundtrack!

Sharing the memories

- The easiest way to share wedding photos with your family and friends is to post them to your personal wedding website (make one at ConnectedWeddings.com). Or try a free photo-share website like zoomin.com or snapfish.com—they'll let you print your photos, make cups and calendars, ship them anywhere in India and abroad. Kodakgallery.com, flickr.com (owned by Yahoo and accessible through any Yahoo email ID) and picasa.com (owned by Google and accessible through any Gmail email ID) don't offer prints (either in India or at all), but let you upload and share photos. Just sign up for an account on the site of your choice, upload your digital pictures, and invite your friends to view them online. Alternately, it's also easy to share photos by posting a digital album to your profile on a social networking site like Orkut or Facebook where your friends are already on.
- Alternately, burn a bunch of the most fun pictures and/or a short video on CDs and distribute to guests. One couple, Kaveri and Anshul, had a friend design a kitschy CD cover with a picture of them hanging on to a gaily coloured auto rickshaw—which was, quirkily, their ride back to their hotel after the wedding.

- If you want to share physical prints, slip a picture or two in with your thank you cards. You could send a shot of the bride and groom, or get more personal and send pictures that include the guests you're thanking.
- Or, design a thank you card with your nicest wedding day image as the cover, like one bride Nisha, a designer and artist from Bangalore, did. Other fun ideas for a thank you note picture: pose for a picture where you and the groom hold up a sign that says 'thank you' on it. Or, if your wedding is fairly intimate, gather all your guests around the bride and groom at some point for a group photo, to be featured on the card.
- You can also make mini albums using handmade paper books, or create your own beautiful albums. When Kavya, a graphic designer from Bangalore, married Samir, she designed albums with brocade covers for themselves and both their families. There were four albums in each set, one for each event in colours that symbolised each function. Green brocade was for the mehendi album, blue brocade for the sangeet (the bride wore blue), red and gold brocade for their Hindu wedding ceremony and white and gold for their Christian wedding blessing and reception. Elaborate but lovely!
- What's better than sharing your pictures? Sharing your video! And what's more fun than watching your wedding video and giggling at the antics of the wedding party by yourself? Making an evening party of it! Sasha was working in TV when she got married, so decided to edit the wedding video herself and then screen it for friends at her house. Do invite both sets of parents and some friends to join, as well, as you relive your wonderful wedding. Make a fun afternoon of it, with music and snacks—the last after-party.
- Also, there's no rule that says you can only include wedding photos. Delhi BPO worker Sugandha made a collage of her courtship with her husband, BPO manager Raaj. Teacher Nazia from Bangalore made a scrapbook of honeymoon memories, including all the tickets, room vouchers, tourist info from their honeymoon.

The Newly-wed Game

Your fairy-tale wedding turned out exactly right but make sure your story ends with a happily ever after. You will get plenty of advice about living with your hubby and his family. So read on for tips on other important topics—sharing your home, your finances, and your first anniversary. You'll be headed for a blissful first year of marriage.

Moving in

If you've found a new love nest together, you've probably already laid claim to the larger cupboard and the nicer side of the bed. But if you're moving into his one-bedroom-hall–kitchen in Bandra and you have more shoes than Imelda Marcos, you may have some serious sifting to do. When Suzanna, an advertising copywriter from Bangalore, first moved into husband Gautam's place, she piled her things into the spare room, and used his room to sleep. They decided to redecorate. 'Both of us agreed on most things, so it turned out to be good fun doing things together,' Suzanna says. It can be enjoyable to redesign a bachelor pad to fit your taste. But, as new bride Sasha warns, 'A new bride should not turn the place upside down, colour the rooms pink and hold stuffed-toy vigils.'

Wardobe wars: How to share your space

* Take stock. Figure out who has how much and what will need closet hanging and drawer space, shoe racks, etc. This is also the perfect time to spring clean.

* Divide up your space. Base decisions on factors like: you've got double the number of shoes he has; or he's way taller than you and can easily reach the high shelves. You may only be winning temporarily if you get all the prime spots. Your hubby might just come home from work every night and toss his clothes on a chair.

* Use all available storage space. Take anything you wear infrequently—heavy saris and suits, sports gear or seasonal wear—and place it at the back of your closet or on high shelves. Invest in boxes that fit under your bed, and add hooks, shelves and even extra hanging rods.

Mind over money

Many couples find it difficult to make the switch to handling finances together. It's easy to find yourselves squabbling if you're not on the same page on issues like:

- Financial dependence of one spouse on another, or of the couple on their families
- How to invest or use jointly owned money or assets
- Prioritising big expenses like buying a home or managing everyday household expenses
- Dealing with commitments like supporting family members
- Settling egos if you're earning more than him

Read on for how to turn, easily, 'what's yours and what's mine' into what's happily ours.

- After your wedding, if you're lucky, you'll have a nice nest egg from the many cash gifts. Start a separate joint account, as many couples do, for household expenses, or for your future. Pick an amount each can spend without asking the other.
- 'Both spouses should maintain individual accounts,' advises Nalini Prabhu, investment consultant and stockbroker with Alacrity Securities and Odyssey Financial Services Limited. In fact, she even suggests splitting household and other expenses down the middle, or proportionate to your incomes; each spouse pays their share from their own account.
- If you're not a career girl, then Prabhu recommends asking your husband (preferably before you're married) to give you a certain sum each month for an individual account. Think of this as your salary for being the fabulous homemaker you are, she reasons.
- Examine larger expenses closely to make sure you agree on a spending and saving strategy. For example, make a savings plan for a new home, your (eventual) children's college funds, retirement, etc., that you can agree to work towards.
- Hire a financial adviser.

Ask the experts

Financial expert Nalini Prabhu shares some tips for newly-weds.

* Before renting a home, which is a dead expense, consider a 100% financed home. Nowadays, many banks don't even insist on a margin. Based on your work history, banks like State Bank of India will work out an EMI for you with a good rate of interest, taking into account your day-to-day living expenses and joint salaries.

* Get insurance in both your names—life plus indemnity. This takes into account the investment yield as well as life assurance.

* Some part of your income should be invested, whether in the stock market or mutual funds. As young people without kids, you can afford to take a little risk. Consult a financial adviser who will tell you how much of your income you should put into the stock market and how much in fixed income yielding securities.

* Take all financial decisions (other than your monthly expenses) jointly.

* 15% of your individual earnings should be saved. To begin with, start with bank accounts, and after a year jump into equity. Dip into these savings only for emergencies. This will guarantee a comfortable retirement for you. With the 85% left over, live within your means.

Keeping the spark alive

It's common for your relationship to feel a bit stagnant once you've gotten into a routine together, especially if you are handling the stresses of work, finances and the new flat you are going to buy. Create special rituals to break the monotony of daily life. Lazy breakfasts in bed on Sundays perhaps, or blissful movie nights. Indulge in goofy anniversaries that will keep the romance alive and disputes at bay; the anniversary of your first kiss, your first date, the first time you said, 'I love you.'

Celebrating your first anniversary—and the ones to come!

Yippee! It's your first anniversary! Celebrate the occasion in your own special way. In the Western tradition, each anniversary is symbolised by a particular gift. You can decide to stick to convention or subvert it with your own funky ideas.

First anniversary: Paper

Give each other subscriptions to fancy design or fashion magazines; buy some expensive, handmade paper stationery and use the first page to write each other love notes; or get married again with paper garlands you can source from a temple bazaar! Paper lamps, shares in a listed company, diaries and an anniversary journal are other great paper anniversary gifts.

Second anniversary: Cotton

Get each other matching soft cotton tees from CK; or splurge on crisp Shyam Ahuja linen for your bed in a pretty floral design. Other ideas—his and her sleepwear, an artistic wall hanging on cloth, or a fabric travel case to hold your jewellery or his toiletries on a trip.

Third anniversary: Leather

Buy him a cool bomber jacket from Hidesign, and steer him towards the new Tods store for an all-day handbag for you; or buy each other lovely jutis from the sidewalk.

Fourth anniversary: Flowers

Decorate the house with marigolds and jasmine flowers intertwined with fairy lights to remember your wedding day; do something flower-oriented in the garden; or make a trip to Holland to see the tulips in springtime.

Fifth anniversary: Wood

Buy a beautiful antique roll-top desk for him, and guys, splurge on an antique dressing table for her; alternatively, join your local 'save the trees' Chipko organisation.

Real-life Wedding Belles Remember Their First Anniversaries

'My husband cooked me dinner and set up the dining room with candles. He also gave me a stunning pair of antique gold earrings!'—Kavya, Bangalore

'Haven't had mine but we're planning a trip to Dubai and probably Egypt. We're planning to do a cruise to one of these places in the summer since that would be the ideal way to celebrate such an occasion, and I would recommend that, rather than having a party yet again and spending more money on hundreds of people.'—Neha, Delhi

'We actually kept it simple and gave each other good gifts. I got a lovely leather jacket and I gave Arvi a huge painting I did myself. We decided to share our first anniversary with a bunch of underprivileged girls from Lisa Home in Hennur—we bought lots of biryani and ate lunch with them. That was worthwhile, we thought and special for sure. At night, we made Maggi noodles and had them with wine on our terrace. So romantic!' —Nisha, Bangalore

'We invited our closest friends and families to our house for dinner. It was lovely, because these were old friends and parents, and everyone had stories about our dating days. And since both of us love cooking, it was a treat to cook for everyone and have them appreciate the food.'—Sasha, Mumbai

Appendix

Vendor listings by city

Here is a listing of vendors recommended by the brides we have interviewed. We've also mentioned some of the more unusual guest accommodation you may not know about. Phone numbers and websites/emails have been given. Go to ConnectedWeddings.com for the full address and for a longer list including hotels and wedding venues.

Delhi

Wedding Planners

Creative Explosions (Neeta Raheja)
2462 3108, 4658 0420,
neetaraheja@gmail.com

FNP Weddings and Events Pvt.. Ltd.
6565 0688–91,
fnp.in/fnp/faces/jsp/wedding.jsp

Karismatik (Saloni Gupta)
9811585536, 2244 0323

Wedding Art by Meher
9811050555
meher.sarid@myoxigen.com
weddingartbymeher.com

The Wedding Design Company
(Vandana Mohan)
4355 4400, 4355 4444, 9810167501
contact@wdcindia.com
wdcindia.com

Stationery Designers

EDC
4155 3228, 4155 3229
info@entertainmentdesignco.com
entertainmentdesignco.com

Heema Sabharwal
9899380780, 9818226046
heemasabharwal@yahoo.com

Poddar Cards
9990099990, 9810058923
info@poddarcards.com
poddarcards.com

Malhotra Card Manufacturers
2323 1766, 2696 7982
malhotracards@hotmail.com
malhotracardmfrs@yahoo.co.in

Misa International
3062 1040, misaintl@yahoo.com

Vivek Sahni Design
4182 3869, 4182 4053
info@viveksahnidesign.com,
sharda@viveksahnidesign.com
viveksahnidesign.com

Guests Accommodation
(Clubs/Serviced Apartments)

Ahuja Residency
193, Golf Links
2462 2255, 2462 3945
info@ahujaresidency.com
ahujaresidency.com

Icon Towers
46 Paschimi Marg, Vasant Vihar
2614 5201, 2614 5204
ysf_icon@rediffmail.com
icon-ysf.com

Jyotsana Swaroop
A-9, 2nd Floor, Nizamuddin East
2627 9111, 9811905544
a9.nizamuddin@gmail.com

Ray-The Indian Experience
(Deepak Kapur)
208A Beverly Park 1,
MG Road, Gurgaon
9811550322
indexperience@gmail.com

Guest Transportation
(Car Services, Other Ideas)

Adscope (Rajeev Mehra)
9811026600,
rajeevitop@gmail.com

Ajay Travel Service
2334 6210, 9810609808
ved@ajaytravels.com
ajaytravels.com

Asian Travel House
2613 0080, 2689 0080
manipal@asiantravelhouse.com
asiantravelhouse.com

Malhotra World Travels
4151 4278, 2751 4166
malhotraworldtravel@yahoo.co.in
indiacar-rental.com

Mann Tours India Pvt. Ltd.
2365 1111, 2358 1111
amrit@indialuxurytours.com
manntours.com

Southern Travels Pvt. Ltd.
4353 2820, 2875 4210, 4353 2828
krishna@southerntravels.com

Mehendi Artists

Raju Mehendiwala
9818282844

Ram Prakash Mehendi Arts
9818002945
Samar Jehan
9811143346

Shri Balaji Pagriwala (Amar Swaroop)
23253940, 2328 3940, 9810137840
Assistance with traditional wares, band and tying of pagris

World Fame Mehendi (Jameela)
9811039746, 9211166799

Party Favours Vendors

Celeste (for chocolates)
4701 0943, 4247 4039, 9810064545
celesteartisan@vsnl.net
celestechocolates.com

Dilli ka Khana (handcrafted Indian sweets)
Gunjan Goela
9811349055, 9212035323
ggoela_in@yahoo.com

Karma Traders (Vipul Gupta)
9811031757
vipulgupta44@gmail.com

Sarama Enterprises (Madhuri Mehra)
9811976600
mehramadhuri13@hotmail.com

Sinfully Yours (for sweets, nuts, hand crafted chocolates, packaged gifts)
2614 9831, 9810074432, 9811603070
rkandhari5@hotmail.com

Sangeet/Cocktail Choreographers

Divay Dua
9810062611, (124) 405 0817
divaydua@hotmail.com

Divya Miglani
9810009697
divyamiglani@gmail.com

Mudra
6536 2202, 9810158683
pandit.harvansh@rediffmail.com

Rajesh Khawla
9810394408, 2462 1239

Rashi Arora
2669 1811, 9818258664
rashiarora86@gmail.com

Suparna Bhushan Sood Dance Studio
(120) 243 2424, 9810061805

Florist/Stage Decorations

Bhai Roshan Lal Raj Kumar
2738 7526, 9810198923

Fascination by Meher
9811050555
meher.sarid@myoxigen.com

Floral Concept (Pooja and Lalit Batra)
4163 1120, 9810496621, 9899515253
poojabatra1108@yahoo.com

New Variety Decorators Pvt. Ltd.
(Rajiv Sood)
2634 0666, 2634 6809
newvarietydecors@yahoo.co.in

Rama Tent House
2437 5026, 2437 1985
ramatent@hotmail.com

Caterers

Cuisine and Concepts Catering Co.
4162 7616
cuisinenconcepts@yahoo.com
cuisinesnconcepts.com
Har Swaroop Man Singh Halwai
2327 6311, 2326 7834
Traditional vegetarian food

Hyatt Regency Delhi's Catering Services
6677 1468
hrdelhi@hyatt.com,
delhi.regency.hyatt.com

SALTT
9811014444, 9810210265
sg@nashaindia.com

Seasons Catering Services
(124) 238 5411, (124) 406 9191,
9818262784
info@seasonsgroup.co.in,
seasonsgroup.co.in

DJs

Family Vision (Angelina)
9971512553
angelina@familyvision.info
familyvision.info
Musicians that are part of a volunteer organisation

Global Sound Management (DJ Gaurav)
9811225230, 4257 6264
gauravmalvai@hotmail.com

Nomad Sound (Vishal Mallick)
9811108121, 9212318121, 4551 5674
vishalmallick@gmail.com
myspace.com/nomadsound
vishalmallick.com

Sound of Music
9811028989
parvez@soundofmusicindia.com
soundofmusicindia.com

Studio Bakers (DJ Rummy)
3291 0470, 3291 0471
admin@djrummy.com
studiobakers@djrummy.com

Photographers/Videographers

Badal Jain Raja Jain
rajabadaljain@gmail.com
info@badalraja.com
badalraja.com

Bajaj Photo World
4172 1797, 9810081134
bajajphotoworld@yahoo.co.in
bajajphotoworld.com

Rama Colour Lab
2613 2361, 2612 3000

Ronicka Vickrant Photography
9811315842,
ronickavickrant@gmail.com

Sephi Bergerson (all over India)
sephi.com/weddings

Studio Prem and Colour Lab
2384 2039, 2384 7810, 2384 4710
studioprem@satyam.net.in
studioprem.com

Spas for Bridal Treatments/Packages

Amaatra
Hotel Ashok, Chanakyapuri
2611 0101

Asian Roots
B-5/15, Safdarjung Enclave,
Opposite Deer Park
4165 1010, 4165 2576,
myasianroots.com

Blossom Kochhar Salon and Spa
6, Pallavi Shopping Complex,
Opposite Taj Palace, Sardar Patel Marg
2611 0982
blossomkochhar@gmail.com
blossomkochharspa.com

Mobile Spa Service
Dev's Farm, Ram Mandir Road,
Vasant Kunj
9899970881, 2612 1662
info@spatransformations.com
spatransformations.com
They'll bring everything to your venue

Radiant Bridal Hues, Espace Salon
MBD Radisson Hotel, Noida
(120) 430 0000

Suparna Trikha
B-24 Nizamuddin East
2435 8051, 2435 5804
suparnatrikha@yahoo.com
Skin and hair treatments recommended

Mumbai

Wedding Planners

Gurleen M. Puri
3250 3314, 9820189494, 9320772661
info@gurleenmpuri.com
gurleenmpuri.com

Knot Forever (Tejal Kadakia)
9820233012
info@knotforever.com
knotforever.com

Occasionz Unlimited (Sneha Tejwani/
Dipa Sheth)
9820081985, 9821325506
occasionz@hotmail.com

Regal-Weddings
Ankit Bhargava: 9314141250 and
Vishv Vijae: 9828057193
info@regal-weddings.com
regal-weddings.com
Especially for palace and beach weddings

Revazz Wedding Planners
(Ratna Malhotra)
9820328441, 9833006668
ratna@revazz.com
rasika@revazz.com
revazz.com

The Wedding Planner (Nikhil Bhide/ Nisha Vaidya)
9820745404, 9833673155,
9820188747, 9920453989
info@nikhilbhide-theweddingplanner.com
nikhilbhide-theweddingplanner.com

Stationery Designers

Chimanlal's Pvt. Ltd.
2207 7717
chimanlals.com

David and Company
Sharaf Manzil, 1st Floor, JSS Road,
Near Metro Cinema, Kalbadevi
2201 9010, 2205 7394

Media Arts Wedding Supplies and Services (Kamlesh J)
2388 3680, 9821008468
kamleshj@vsnl.com

Parekh Cards India (Nilesh Parekh)
2684 2612 ,weddingcards@vsnl.net
parekhcards.com

Shantilal and Sons (Mihir Kadakia)
2383 6905, 9821349088
mihir@shantilal-sons.com
shantilal-sons.com

Shastri Wedding Card
27, Kunj 1, Corner of Andheri-Kurla Road and Old Nagardas Road
2683 7357

Guests Accommodation (Clubs/Serviced Apartments)

Executive Enclave
331, Dr Ambedkar Road,
Pali Hill, Bandra (W)
6696 9000, 2649 0227
executiveenclave.com

Guest Transportation (Car Services, Other Ideas)

Autoriders International Limited
6677 7394/95/97, 6694 4059
autoriders.net

Mani Selvaraj
Bandra: 2659 2880,
Andheri: 2832 7750
Colaba: 6570 1691, 9987034014

Hertz Cars on Rent
6570 1692/3, 9967148000, 9967158000
mumbai@carsonrent.com
opsmom@carsonrent.com
carsonrent.com

Orion Cars (Sachin Kumar)
6506 1552, 9820225141
contact@orioncars.com
orioncarsonline.com

Raza Motors (Sayed Khursheed Alam)
2215 1821, 9892014897

VG Agencies (Praveen Gupta)
9867074477, 9322234472
vgagencies@gmail.com

Mehendi Artists

Brahmadevi Sharma and Deepa
2386 7861, 9820222241

Jayshree Doshi
2382 5708, 2387 2811, 9322236805

Komal Thakkar
6635 7080, 9869308910
mehendi4u00@yahoo.com

Usha Shah and Ekta Kansara
23692976, 2368 0619, 9821121221
ekta@mehendiart.com
mehendiart.com

Veena Nagda
2345 5785, 9820421717
veena@veenabollywoodmehendi.com
veenabollywoodmehendi.com

Party Favours Vendors

Candles N More
(for customised candles and other giveaways)
Priya Ahuja, 9892735368
candelsnmore@yahoo.co.in

Celebrations Fine Confections
(fine chocolates)
Mehernosh Khajotia
9821122290, info@celebrationsfc.com
celebrationsfc.com

Mehta Bangles
(bangle wholesaler)
JP Mehta or Jaywant Mehta
9821040715, 9820382789,
22428937/8057
mehtabangles85@hotmail.com

Mystic Package Emporium
Nisha Shah (by appointment only)
9820064742, 2363 1153, 2364 1156
nishooshah@gmail.com

Sangeet/Cocktail Choreographers

Aanchal Gupta (Arts in Motion)
9820380009, 9820183231
artsinmotion@gmail.com
artsinmotiononline.com

Ila Dalal
2288 2522, 9833808341
illajdalal1805@yahoo.co.in

Monica Raheja
9820309388, 2204 5693, 2204 9189
(prefers calls on mobile)
monzraheja3374@hotmail.com

Rekha Solanki and
Reshma Vijayakar
9820218262, 2351 1322

Sandip Soparrkar
(Latin and varied styles)
9819361074, 9820776423
sandipsoparrkar@rediffmail.com
ballroomindia.com

Terence Lewis Contemporary Dance
Company (Angela)
9820086546
tenterence@gmail.com
terencelewis.com

Florist/Stage Decorations

Dreamz Events N Ideas
2241 4926
vasudha@dreamzevents.com
dreamzevents.com

The Flower Shop
Dev Chhayas, St. Anthony Road,

Chembur
2521 0388

Gayatri Flowers
2242 0494, 9821801825

Perfect Décor and Ferns n Petals
Nitinn Raichooda
2527 6672, 2527 6662, 9819659222
weddingdecorators.com

Rosetta Florists
113/15 Wodehouse Road, Colaba,
2215 1170

Shree Kripa Caterers and Decorators
(Ketan Shroff)
* Vile Parle Medical Club, Juhu Scheme, Vile Parle(W)
* Vibgyor High School, Motilal Nagar, Link Road, Goregaon(W)
9869044943, 9323802901

Stagekraft Entertainment Ltd.
(Vijay Chafekar)
No. 1, Mont Desire, Perry Cross Road, Opposite masjid, Off Turner Road, Bandra (W)
9320240666, 26423918

Vazir Bux and Company
Shop #1, Raja Market, New Nagardas Road, Andheri (E)
2822 5445, 9323463193, 9324567779

Caterers

Catering and Allied
6635 6908, 6654 7700
farrokh@cateringandallied.com

Delhi Darbar
2308 5656, 2308 3333
jafferbhaisdelhidarbar.com

Kailash Parbat Catering Services
22831913

Shree Kripa Caterers and Decorators
(For western suburbs see adjacent column)

Thackers Caterer
2364 9300, 2364 9301

DJs

DJ Akbar Sami
9820080992, 2600 2428 (contact via mobile is preferred)
deejayakbarsami@hotmail.com

DJ Akhtar
9820046665

DJ Aqeel
9820069110

DJ Clement
9833515815

DJ Suketu
9833059545
djsuketu@gmail.com

DJ Manish
9892022420

Photographers/Videographers

Atul Joshi
9820257620

Ganpat Sawant
9324727570, 2421 3190

Manndeep Bagle
9870460602, 9920308979
mann_manndeep@yahoo.com

Milind Ketkar
9892459535, 2446 5573
ketkarmilind@hotmail.com
milindketkar.com

Parikshit Suri
9867189997, 9321189997
suripeekay@gmail
pksuri.com

Spas for Bridal Treatments/Packages

Aquamarine Day Spa
202, Patel House, 2nd Floor, Bomanji Petit Road, Kemp's Corner
2381 1118/9

Blush
* 109 Om Chambers, Kemp's Corner
2368 2255, 2363 8699
* Bungalow No. 6, 18 Khar Danda Road, Khar (W)
6704 2425–8, 2636 1578
*Sundervan Complex, Near Lokhandwala, Andheri (W)
2636 1578

Club Oasis Fitness Centre and Spa
Grand Hyatt, Off Western Express Highway, Santacruz (E)
6676 1234

Franck Provost Salon and Spa
*2nd, 3rd and 4th Level,
Aryston Centre,
Opposite JW Marriott Hotel,
Juhu Road, Juhu
6702 1440, 67036971
*1st level, Landmark,
Pali Danda Road, Bandra (W)
6703 6971
franckprovost-india.com

Jiva Grande and Spa
33 Nathalal Parikh Marg,
Taj Wellington Mews, Colaba
66569494, tajhotels.com

Moksh, The Wellness Place
Opposite the American Consulate,
Breach Candy
2361 0221, 2367 6990
mokshonline.com
Myrah
Binoli Palm Spring Society, JVPD
Scheme
2625 3968

Quan
JW Marriott, Juhu
6693 3000

Rudra Health and Spa
Kemp's Boulevard, Kwality House,
Kemp's Corner
2387 2530/5909

Sva Spa and Salon
Gauri Kunj, Kishore Kumar Ganguly
Marg, Juhu Tara Road, Juhu
2660 7326/28/68
svaspasalon.com

Bangalore

Wedding Planners

Aroma Wedding Planners(Rolent Paul)
2838 0832, 9448374469, 9448820175

CHE
Seema Jaisingh
9845077065
cheexperience.com
PHASE1 Events and Entertainment
(Nafisa)
9945193811
nafisa@phase1world.com

Rings and Roses (Christopher/
Rosemary Ratnam)
For inter-community and

inter-nationality weddings
2551 2847, 9844025240
ringsandroses.in

TJ Wedding Planners
(Tina/Joel)
9945633033, 9845481428
tjweddingplanners@yahoo.co.in

Vinay Kewalramani
#64, 6th Main, Defence Colony,
Indiranagar
9886406942
vinaykewalramani@gmail.com

Stationery Designers

Belaku Trust (Women's NGO)
Baneen, 9886506332
belakutrust.org

Diorama Design (Nidhi/Milan)
3296 9053, 9901917714
diorama-design.com

Exit Design (Karn Malhotra)
9845522281, 4151 9267
info@exitdesign.in
exitdesign.in

Judge Press (Mr Chandramouli)
2221 1168, 2224 0561
judgepress@gmail.com

Smita Sajnani
9845020432
smitasajnani.com

Guests Accommodation
(Clubs/Serviced Apartments)

Bangalore Club (through members)
Field Marshal K.M. Cariappa Road
4022 0000, 2227 3605
bangaloreclub.com

The Bride Corporate Suites
No. 5 Bride Street,
Richmond Town
4114 4408
bridesuites.com

Orchard Suites
Sankey Road, Sarjapur Road,
Infantry Road, Koramangala
4123 4444, 4123 4333, 9945565950
theorchardsuites.com

Shilton Suites
2, Ulsoor Road (behind The Oberoi)

4113 8777, 4151 2148
shiltonhotels.com

Umerkot Residency (Neel Sengupta)
30, 80 Feet Road, ST Bed, Koramangala
9845493690
Also contact for other serviced apartments

Guest Transportation (Car Services, Other Ideas)
Easy drive (Syed)
9341916583
FasttrackTaxis
2333 7777

Meru Cabs
4422 4422
merucabs.com

Suresh Taxi
9845519268

Mehendi Artists
Ayesha and Reshma
9880243781

Nalini Behn
2336 9168, 9845191685

Seema Divecha
9243126568

Party Favours Vendors
Archies Gallery
*Brigade Road
2558 4222
*Commercial Street
2558 8961

Arihant Plaza (for naughty gifts and novelty lingerie)
Kamaraj Road, Opposite the Entrance to Commercial Street

Bangle and Bindi Shops
* Ulsoor Market
* Malleswaram
* Commercial Street
* Chikpet/Mamulpet
* Gujjri Market (Opposite Russel Market, Shivajinagar where you get junk, recycled stolen goods and automobile parts)

Sangeet/Cocktail Choreographers
Lourd Vijay Dance Company
2331 5566, 9845239123
Especially known for salsa expertise

Rock Around The Clock Dance Company
(Prithvi)
9342508667,9980008667, 4167 7855,
2546 5506
info@rockaroundtheclock.biz
rockaroundtheclock.biz
Swing/jiving, as well as Bollywood

Tarantismo (Arati Punwani)
9886074174
tarantismo.cdc@gmail.com
Bollywood, belly dancing and jazz

XLNC Dance Company (Sanjay)
3093 3855, 9844073315/9880286888
sanjayxlnc@gmail.com,xlncdance.com

The Yana Lewis Dance Company (Gita)
3241 1051, yldc.in
Classical ballet and jazz ballet
performances for weddings

Florist/Stage Decorations
Daffodils
(flowers and favours)
(Dr Norma Prabhu/Patricia D'Souza)
2559 1560, 2558 3607, 9886075448
daffodilsflorist.in

Jan and Co. (Altaf Jan Mohammed)
2558 1376

Nalesa (Geethanjali)
9844107989, 4115 0480, 2535 8379

Petal Talks (Kalpana Rajaram)
4113 3311, petaltalks@gmail.com

Som Decorators (Ashutosh)
9945018880

Caterers
Anisa Siraj of The Party Givers
9845878300
contact@avenueinc.net
everhome@gmail.com
incavenue.com/catering.html

Biryani (Anna Minocher)
2225 4633, 9845015473
anna_minocher@hotmailcom
indyrao@gmail.com
South Indian food with emphasis on
coastal cuisines. Also Parsi,
European, Mediterranean and Thai.

Gangotree (chatwallah for mehendi)
2226 8484

James Ho (Chinese)
9448077488

Swathi Caterers
91 3292 1516
service@swathicaterers.com
swathicaterers.com
Chinese, Continental, Thai, north Indian, south Indian, Mangalorean. Will also help with venues, decoration, getting a priest to officiate, and musicians.

Swati Kishore
9341307405
For Mangalorean and other Indian food

Bartenders

Jaykumar
Turnkey School of Bar and Beverage Solutions
9845999737, jayaru2003@yahoo.com

Joseph (freelance bartender)
2521 9716

Tulleeho(Prashant Abraham)
prashant@tulleeho.com
tulleeho.com

DJs

DJ Jasmeet
9845069900, djjasmeet.com

DJ Hussain
9886184427

DJ Arun
9880275192

Acme Events (Geo)
9980004606, 4110 6500

DJ Chico
9845019092

Musicians

2667 2049
Nadaswaram (the south Indian version of the shehnai)

Rahul Pophali (tabla)
9845447256
tablarahul.com

Shyam and the West Wind (live band)
9845225566

Hitesh Mehta
9845024772
info@hiteshmehta.net,
hiteshmehtaandparty@gmail.com
hiteshmehta.net
Live music group that performs
Bollywood, ghazals, dandiya, bhangra

Ahmed Bhai
(live singer performing film songs)
9916703749

Photographers/Videomen

Deepak Chhabria
9845272838,shootdeepak@gmail.com

Foto Shooter (Kavee Arasan)
9880321113
arasan_kavee@yahoo.com
High-tech video and photos

Foto Tech
Gerard Santamaria
9845181338
foto_tech2@yahoo.co.in

GK Vale
Online@gkvale.com
gkvale.com

niz4u.com (Pasha)
97311 19199
info@niz4u.com, niz4u.com

Sabarish
9845005658, shabri27@yahoo.co.in

Spas for Bridal Treatments/Packages

Angsana Oasis Spa
Doddaballapur Main Road,
Addevishwanathapura Village,
Rajankunte
2846 8892-96, angsana.com

Aroma Garden
1305, 10th Main, Jeevan Bhima Nagar
Main Road, HAL 3rd Stage
2535 2652

Ayurveda Gram Heritage Wellness
Centre
Hemmandana Halli,
Samethanahalli Post
6565 1090
ayurvedagram.com

Kaya Skin Clinic
Priya Pradeep
G - 04, Prestige Meridian 1,

MG Road, Bangalore.
Also in in Vyalikaval, Indiranagar,
Jayanagar and more.
6661 1005 / 6
kayaclinic.com

The Leela Spa
The Leela Palace,
23 Airport Road
2521 1234

Shreyas Retreat
Santoshima Farm,
Gollahalli Gate,
Neelamangala
2773 7102, 2773 7103, 2773 7183
shreyasretreat.com

Space
70, Cunningham Road,
Opposite Embassy Woods
4132 7526
spacethespa.com

Index

B
Bride style quiz, 65–66
Bridal showers, 142–43

Budgets
Funding, 32–34
  Liquidating assets for, 35
  Pre-wedding parties 117
  Setting of, 31–45

C
Cards, 53, 216–19
  Designing and printing, 216–19
  Despatching and delivering, 217
Also see Stationary
Caterers, 182–85, 206–07
Ceremonies
  Eve of wedding, 158–60
  Wedding day, 160

D
Dance choreographers, 220–23
Decorations, 175–81
Decorators, 203–05, *also see Florists*
Destination weddings, 52

DJ
  Booking, 224–26
  Planning with, 226

E
Engagement, 123–28

F
Favours
  Hen party, 140
  Vendors, 231–32
Family members
  Roles in your wedding, 23–26
Fitness, 105–09
Florists, 203–05, *also see Decorators*
Footwear, 81

G
Gifts
  Shopping, giving, receiving, 189–94
  Wish lists of, 190–91
Guest list, 48-50, 117–20
Guests, outstation
  Hosting of, 59–62
  Save-the-date notices to, 53, 217
  Welcoming of, 18

H
Hairstyles, 101–05
Haldi, 157
Hen parties, 129–41
  Favours, 140
Home
  Settling into, 256–58
Honeymoons
  Destinations for, 234–42
  Packing for, 241

I
Invitations
  Designing, 53–7, 216–19
  Despatching, 217

J
Jewellery, 90–97

L
Lingerie, 82–89
    Size, selecting, 84–85
    Trends, 84
    Vocabulary, 88–89
Look calendar, 98–99

M
Marriage
  Anniversaries, 261
  Registration of, 170
Mehendi
  Artists, 227–30
  Costs of, 228
  Party, 144–48
  Tips for, 228–30

N
Names
  Changing after marriage, 249–51
Newly-wed life
  Finances, 258-9
  Keeping the spark alive, 259
  Moving in, 256–57

O
Outfits, 67–100
  Fittings with tailor, 76–78
  Planning, 70–78
  Also see Trousseau

P
Photography and video, 186–88, 208–10
Photos, viewing and sharing, 252–55
Post-Wedding
  To-do list, 245–55

Changing your name, 249–51
Thank you notes, 245–48
Wedding pictures and videos, 252–55
Pre-Wedding
Looks, 120–22
Parties, 115–62
Themes, 135–41

R

Registration of wedding, 170
Rituals, 165–69

S

Sangeet, 118, 149–55
Shopping, 74–75
Skincare, 110–14
Stationery, 54-56, 216-19

T

Thank you notes, 245–48
Trousseau, 67–100

V

Vendors
Booking of, 195–232
For favours, 231–32
Interviewing, 197
Listings, 262–85
Responsibilities of, 195–232
Working with, 198–99
Venue
Identifying and booking, 200–03
Short listing, 52
Types, 173–74
Videographers, 208–10

W

Wedding
Anniversaries, 261
Ceremony, 165–72
Countdown, to-do list, 15–20
Date for, identifying, 45–46
Destinations, 51–52
Dreams, 9
Emergency kit, 100
Legalities, 170
Movies, 10–11
Planners, 212–14
Planning, 27–62
Type, suitable for you, 13–14
Vision, 9–14

A note on the *Wedding Belles* team

Ameeta Sharma is a Delhi-based freelance writer and columnist whose features on lifestyle subjects appear regularly in magazines such as *Vivaha, Bride and Style, Timeless Jewels, Diamond World, Swagat, Woman's Era* and others. Ameeta loves fine wine and good food and travelling.

Priya Pathiyan has been writing in the lifestyle space for the last decade. After a seven-year stint with the *Sunday Times of India*, she's currently Editor of *Mother and Baby Magazine*. Priya lives in south Mumbai and has a passion for dance, travel and food.

Ruchika Chanana is a theatre practitioner and writer who lives, works and plays in Bangalore. She runs a content consulting company, Words etc., and has a team of whimsical writers who provide constant merriment and inspiration. Ruchika is a devotee of yoga and a complete stranger to maths.

Stacy Kerzner is a writer, editor and media entrepreneur who splits her time between India and Washington DC. Stacy and her husband Dan are the founders of the website ConnectedWeddings.com. Previously Stacy developed programming for the Discovery Channel. Stacy is a lover of vegetarian food, travel, consuming all forms of media and, naturally, attending weddings.

Sephi Bergerson is a documentary photographer based in Delhi since 2002. He has been photographing Indian weddings for the last few years.

A note on ConnectedWeddings.com

Join the team from *Wedding Belles* online at our website! If you loved reading all of the wedding planning advice, you'll want to check out ConnectedWeddings.com for our expanded content and tools designed to make being a bride more fun. Our easy-to-use, free online features include:

* Personal wedding websites: Use our beautiful, professional looking website templates to share all of your wedding details and photos with your family and friends.

* Facebook integration that makes wedding planning more fun: Our wedding websites and planning tools are all designed to make your social network work for you.

* iPhone tools to coordinate your plans: Use our iPhone application to view your personal wedding website, manage tasks from your iPhone, and spin our 'Bridal Decider' wheel for fun help making decisions.

* Online task list manager: Customise our extensive list of wedding planning tasks to get organised and stay on top of everything you need to do to plan your wedding.

* Online guest list manager: Keep track of your guests' contact information, who's coming for which events, and all of your gifts and thank you notes.

* New and updated advice from the *Wedding Belles* editorial team: More stories from real brides, great photos to help you get ideas, wedding planning tips from top vendors, and advice on how to save money but not compromise on style.

* Expanded vendors listings: Our appendix of top wedding vendors recommended by the brides we've interviewed, with more information online.

* Discuss and collaborate with other brides like you. Join our forums to share stories and questions with other brides who are in the thick of planning the big day, too!

www.ConnectedWeddings.com